GRACELAND

A COLLECTION OF SONGS

DISCUSSION STARTERS

& BIBLE STUDIES

ABOUT THE JOURNEY FROM LOST TO FOUND

Tim McLaughlin

Youth Specialties

ZONDERVAN™

WWW.ZONDERVAN.COM

Graceland: A Collection of Songs, Discussions Starters, and Bible Studies about the Journey from Lost to Found

Copyright © 2003 by Youth Specialties

Youth Specialties Books, 300 South Pierce Street, El Cajon, CA 92020, are published by Zondervan Publishing House, 5300 Patterson Aveune SE, Grand Rapids, MI 49530

Library of Congress Cataloging-in-Publication Data

McLaughlin, Tim, 1951-
  Graceland : a collection of songs, discussion starters, and Bible
studies about the journey from lost to found / by Tim McLaughlin.
       p. cm.
  ISBN 0-310-25135-4 (pbk.)
  1. Christian education of young people.   I. Title.
  BV1485 .M22 2003
  268'.433–dc21

2002155551

Web site addresses listed in this book were current at the time of publication. Please contact Youth Specialties via e-mail (YS@YouthSpecialties.com) to report URLs that are no longer operational and replacement URLs if available.

Edited by Sally Corran

Cover and interior design by Brian Smith

Printed in the United States of America

03 04 05 06 07 / / 10 9 8 7 6 5 4 3 2 1

GRACELAND

To Cheri, with whom grace is a daily adventure.

Contents

What this grace stuff is all about

A classic definition of grace is *unmerited favor*—i.e., you don't deserve something this good, but you get it anyway. This is all fine and good and undoubtedly accurate, but listen for more than three minutes to someone explaining grace and your eyeballs start glazing over, your mind meanders into your memory of that amazing scene in *Grand Canyon* you watched again just last night where Mary McDonnell's character says to her Kevin Kline husband, "It is inappropriate to have a headache in the presence of a miracle," which reminds you of *The Green Mile* when the mountainous prisoner John Coffey reached through the bars and—

Oh, yeah...we're talking about grace, aren't we? Well, you can see the problem. Which may be why when Jesus talked about grace, he told stories about it rather than *explained* it. He apparently preferred to illustrate it, not explicate it. You can see this all through the Gospels, from Jesus' life as well as from his stories: his parable of the Prodigal Son...his habit of dropping into a bar or bistro for a drink and a deli sandwich with his socially unsavory pals...and generally going out of his way to stick it to the religious leaders of his day, instead favoring the unlovely, the diseased, the unrighteous, the criminal.

And sometimes, apart from stories or someone's actual behavior, you can best see what something is by figuring out what it's *not*. What is grace not? Loud and clear God speaks through dozens of women and men in the Bible: grace is not about you. You don't earn it, you *can't* earn it. You can't negotiate for it, can't buy shares of it on NASDAQ, can't find it on the black market, can't download it, can't pirate it, can't hack into it. You will never score high enough in anybody's book to deserve it.

The flip side, though, is what really steams the brain: no one is beyond grace, either, if we're to believe what the Bible says. Go ahead and quote all of the very valid verses about hell you want—but just remember that nothing can stop a hell-bent person from accepting God's grace just steps, moments, or heartbeats outside hell's doors. Once you're in, you're in—but until you're in, nothing's certain. And if we believe what we say about God loving everyone, and not wanting anyone to spend an eternity apart from him, then for all we know God takes special delight in these last-minute episodes of grace offered and (finally) received.[*]

Grace is a leveler. Slit the throats of a million warriors, women, and children, as Genghis Khan did in his continent-wide rampage across southern Asia, and you are no further from grace than a saintly reformer or pope or evangelist. (In fact, part of what makes a reformer or pope or evangelist genuinely saintly is their nagging knowledge that they are no nearer to grace than Genghis Khan, Adolf Hitler, or Arthur Andersen.)

This is the mystical, scandalous, otherworldly world of grace.

---

[*] If you think such eleventh-hour conversions are highly unfair to all of us who spend entire lifetimes trying our darnedest to obey God, I can only refer you to Jesus' story of the Prodigal Son (or Lost Son, Luke 15:11-31), to his parable of the day laborers (Matthew 20:1-16), and to classic Christian theology, which posits that God exists outside of time. Stew on that one for a while.

Lost And Found and its music

Lost And Found is two men (Michael Bridges and George Baum), a guitar, and a piano (not an electronic keyboard, mind you, but a real piano, complete with soundboard, wire strings, felt hammers, tuning pegs—you know the type). They plead guilty to writing and playing in the genre of *speedwood*—a tag that alludes to the acousticity of their instruments and the tempo at which the two musicians are known to play them.

Helpful descriptions are difficult to come by for this group. Lost And Found's repertoire has no shortage of Jesus songs, but you can't exactly say it's *worship* music...think Isaac Watts meets Billy Crystal. The lyrics may be about the Holy City, but the delivery can sound straight out of Brooklyn. They write some poignant ballady stuff, too, and have a way of inserting it at just the right places in their live sets, with lyrics that wipe the grin off your face and put if not the weight of the world on your shoulders, then at least the weight of one or two people you know who need Jesus and your love.

In performance Lost And Found seems to delight at blurring the distinction between performer and audience. Go hear them live with your group, and you'll be singing (or clapping, chanting, jumping, or stomping) nearly as much as the pair onstage do. Buy a Lost And Found CD at the concert and play it at youth group now and then, and your students will probably slip back into that ol' participatory habit, and hoot and holler with the song 'til a besuited representative of the Ambassadors class upstairs appears in the doorway and glares at you with a *shush* gesture.

Lost And Found is on the Web at speedwood.com, where you can find out more about the band, their concert schedule, CDs, and all sorts of intriguing stuff.

About this curriculum

CD included—its 7 songs are the backbone of the 7 sessions.

Of course, you don't need to buy a CD, because there's one included in this curriculum—7 songs, each one a springboard to a teaching session about a different aspect of grace. The lyrics to each song appear at the top of its respective session. Play the song before the start of each session.

Not linear, but rather a grab-bag. Teach it straight through if you must, but the beauty is scavenging what you need for your own lessons on grace.

Now about these sessions: this is not your typical linear curriculum (a game, a Bible study, a talk, maybe some discussion, a closing—and in that order, thank you). Instead each session in *Graceland* offers you one or two *resource clusters*, whose elements you can use as-is, tweak a bit, pick and choose from, or overhaul entirely for your own purposes to fit the unique nature and needs of your youth group.

Heart of session: the "essay" and its teaching points.

The heart of each session is an essay sort of thing—call it a *lesson* if you want—that just might hold as much insight for some teachers as it will for students. Running alongside each lesson is a column of *teaching points* (just like you see to the left of these paragraphs) that summarize the lesson in a neat and convenient way—so that after you read it yourself, a glance at these teaching points will guide you through the lesson when you're in front of your students.

The kind of lesson elements are common enough, but they have an edge. And no Godtalk.

The elements or components of the resource clusters are not particularly exotic: they're your basic activities (but they're intelligent, not cheesy), talks (with an edge, and no "Godtalk"), Bible studies (as provocative as they are accessible to any kind of student), and discussion starters (whose questions are often the ones everyone's thinking about, but no one's asking).

However you use the stuff of this curriculum, read a session through before teaching it. Please.

Any one activity can give students a very interesting half hour or so. So be deliberate about where in the session you want to spend time.

These resource clusters are a grab-bag, not a prescribed order of service. For instance, if you're an experienced youth worker, you'll probably scavenge only an item or two from a cluster to fill out your own lesson. If you're a Sunday school teacher with a day job, on the other hand, you may want simply to teach your way through the cluster—which you can pretty much do. (But please, oh please, at least read the session through before class!)

The beauty of all these video clips, scripts, Bible studies, and discussion starters is how, under the facilitation of an experienced teacher or youth leader, they can blossom into stand-alone, 45-minute sessions all by themselves—especially with a group of teenagers who are comfortable with each other, who trust each other, who relish talking about life and God, about how their divorced parents are getting along (or not), about how their volleyball practice or play rehearsal went that day.

By the way, you can take all this tweak-this-and-customize-that to the max, since crucial elements from all seven sessions are posted on the Youth Specialties Web site (www.YouthSpecialties.com/store/downloads). Surf to that address, type in the password ("found"), and you'll have access to the Bible study and lyric portions of the book—all customizable. Copy and paste them into your own word processor, then edit to your heart's content—add, remove, or replace Bible passages, discussion questions, anything. After all, you know your students best.

Out of Your Hands

H - O - L - Y

Gonna make us H-O-L-Y
Gonna make us H-O-L-Y by his son
How's he gonna do that to us?

1. Not by my strength, but by his power,
Not when I fight, but by what God has won.
Not by my look, but by his love,
Not by myself, but by his son
Oh, you know God is gonna make us all

2. Not by my choice, but by his choosing
Not when I plan, but when the Spirit comes
Not by my deeds, but by his doing
Not by myself, but by his son

3. Not by a circumcision, but by his decision
Not by my work, but by what he has done
Not by my deeds, but by his doing
Not by myself, but by his son

Free Words

For each clue below, the answer is a word or short phrase that includes the word *free* or a form of *free*. Read the clues one at a time to your group, and let the kids respond. If they are gonzo-competitive, pit one team against another. (Some clues have second parts following ellipses—offer these only if no one guesses the answer with the first clue alone.)

- high-speed road without tolls   *[freeway]*

- lazy person who lives off the generosity of others   *[freeloader]*

- a saying meaning "Everything costs something"...with reference to a meal *[There's no free lunch]*

- Orca movie   *[Free Willy]*

- patriotic guerillas...commandos who fight against dictators *[freedom fighters]*

- in some sports, when you make up your own moves or routines *[freestyle]*

- a voice-activated phone system   *[hands-free]*

- '60s song and movie...set on the African savannah   *[Born Free]*

- a small or trivial item that doesn't cost you anything   *[freebie]*

- not having any support; alone   *[freestanding]*

- a loan without a fee   *[interest-free]*

- randomly connecting ideas   *[free association]*

- computer programs you don't have to pay for   *[freeware]*

Not by my strength...Not by circumcision

In this resource cluster:

- Why we insist on trying to earn grace...circumcision as an example of this...and why grace is such a scandal... plus teaching points *(Grace and Human Rites)*

- Two Bible studies: Zechariah 4 *(Catch These ZZs, page 18)* and Ephesians 2 *(Amazing Grace, page 20)*

- Discussion-starting Qs *(Talk about unearned grace)*

teaching points

Grace and Human Rites

Why humans are driven to try to earn grace.

However unattainable grace is by our own efforts, and however exclusively it is God's free gift to us—still, humans seem unable to resist the urge to earn it, deserve it, work for it, or barter for it.

Even ancient Israel slid into this thinking, about circumcision—this peculiar male rite that was *the* physical sign of Jewishness from the beginning. Circumcision may have become mainstream medical practice by the mid-20th century, but the Jewish religious practice of circumcision—or *bris*, as Judaism calls it today—is rite, not pediatrics.

To ancient Jews, the rite of circumcision gradually became a primary grace-earner (or so it was thought).

Christianity was sowed, rooted, and cultivated in the rich soil of Judaism. Jesus was a Jew, he spent his life in a Jewish province among Jews, he was raised a Jew and most likely educated as a Jew. His followers were primarily Jews. After Jesus' departure his Jewish followers continued their habit of meeting in the synagogue. In those early years Christianity was little more than the "Jesus sect" of Judaism.

And circumcision quickly became a point of controversy, thanks to the apostle Paul. He reported to the Twelve (that is, to the original dozen disciples intimate with Jesus—with Judas Iscariot's replacement, of course) that God had told him to switch audiences, from Jews to Gentiles—non-Jews. This must have been difficult to hear for Jews, who were raised with a 1,500-year legacy of Israel as God's Chosen People and of Gentiles as the outsiders—uncircumcised Philistines, a bunch of pork-eating sinners.

In the early church tensions between Jewish and non-Jewish Christians centered on circumcision.

It got worse. Paul also informed the Twelve in Jerusalem that God was bringing Gentiles into the family of faith *without circumcision*. God's grace, Paul argued, was free and therefore available apart from any ritual, even if *God* had instituted the ritual.

Whoa. This shook the Jewish community in Jerusalem to its core. To accept Gentiles into the Jewish family of faith was hard enough, but doable, providing the Gentile converts kept the Mosaic law as the Jews did—the kosher food laws, cleanliness laws, circumcision, and all the rest. But no way could Gentiles be spiritual equals if they didn't follow God's law as Moses gave it. To think otherwise was a slap in the face of Judaism.

The Council of Jerusalem put the argument to rest— officially, at least.

It took a summit conference for the Twelve to hash out this issue and finally agree with Paul on the main points of his claim (though the final decision was something of a compromise with the legalistic faction).

Still, if one is to judge from Paul's New Testament letters to various Mediterranean churches, circumcision stubbornly hung on for a long time as the sign of a *real* Christian, despite the apostle's arguments—some fiercely passionate, others tightly logical—why uncircumcised Gentile Christians were entitled to the same rights, privileges, and benefits that were available to Jewish Christians. Into Christ's church, Paul maintained, Jewish converts were welcome, along with their long list of requirements and prohibitions; into that same church uncircumcised Greeks were also welcome, along with their—well, ritelessness. A Jewish Christian was free to follow her Jewish conscience—but she definitely was *not* to impose her conscience on anyone else. The law of love is the only law the church recognizes, the apostle wrote. It welcomes in all who desire Christ, and constrains members of Christ's family to treat each other according to it.

What ought to rule the church, Paul wrote, is the law of love, not of circumcision or of any other rite.

Why we're uncomfortable with grace

If it's not one thing, it's another. The first century's religious leaders in Judea were scandalized to hear the working class tell miracle stories about yet another messiah out of—"Get this," they said, rolling their eyes—Nazareth, of all places. You might as well expect the queen of England to be born and raised in Appalachia. As if that weren't enough, they were miffed about being marginalized by Jesus—them, marginalized!—what with all his "last shall be first" talk.

Jesus was a scandal to the religious leaders of his day, who wrote the list of what it takes to earn holiness—and who resented Jesus telling everyone otherwise...

No wonder Jesus' death was engineered by religious leaders.

Roll forward a few centuries. As Rome had gradually become one large slum, to the east Constantinople was thriving in the fourth century as the cultural, spiritual, and economic center of Europe. A new center of Christianity, new church leaders, and new must-do, man-made additions to God's grace. It wasn't good enough merely to want Jesus more than anything else because you had worn your life down to the nubs without him, or because you had everything but still knew you had nothing that really counted.

...and religious leaders ever since have been writing their own lists: the Eastern church did it...

No, that wasn't enough: you had to agree to a creed that explained in detail how it was that Christ was God. If you believed that Christ was indeed God, but in a different way from what the creed stipulated, you were pronounced a heretic and tossed out of the church on your ear.

And grace has had no easier a time since then. Roman Catholic leaders, Protestant leaders, reformers, revivalists, priests, pastors—most of them have required "acts of righteousness" tacked onto grace before God will accept you (they said). To be considered a *real* Christian, you must believe *and* agree that the Pope can infallibly speak the words of God...or believe *and* be baptized in water (it's not enough to just believe the right things)...or believe *and* be baptized by immersion (it's not enough to be baptized by mere sprinkling or pouring)...or believe *and* agree that all Catholics (or Protestants or Muslims or Jews) are going to hell...or believe *and* join the Tory political party (because everyone knows that no *real* Christian could be a Whig)...or believe *and* shun taverns, dance halls, and card rooms (which quickly became abstinence from alcohol and tobacco, and prohibitions against dancing and poker—yes, even in your own home)...or believe *and* tolerate no short hair on women nor long hair on men...or believe *and* oppose abortion or capital punishment...or believe *and* sympathize with Israel against the infidel Palestinians.

You get the point.

Do we *really* believe in salvation by faith alone (the rallying cry of the Reformation, not to mention of the New Testament)? Or do we overlay God's simple, scandalous grace with our cultural and political beliefs, or even with our own confident understanding of what the Bible means—and all but smother grace in the process?

For it is by grace you have been saved, through faith—and this not from yourselves, it is the gift of God—not by works, so that no one can boast. (Ephesians 2:8-9)

...the Catholic and Protestant churches did it...

...and whatever "This Makes You Holy" list is in vogue today inevitably (and wrongly) includes cultural and political requirements, too.

Do we smother grace with our own modern list of "How to Earn Grace"?

Grace is free!

"Not by might nor by power, but by my Spirit,"
says the Lord Almighty.

Read Zechariah 4:1-10. If you're feeling brave, just plunge on into it. But be warned: to Bible scholars, this is Xtreme Prophecy. Weird stuff galore. You may want to skim the following before (or after) reading the Zechariah passage.

WHAT'S HAPPENED UP TILL NOW	About 70 years before the events in this book of prophecy, Jerusalem had been sacked, burned, and bulldozed by Nebuchadnezzar's infantry. Most of its inhabitants were massacred; the survivors were forcibly relocated to Babylon. Now, 70 years later, nearly 50,000 Jews are actually back in Judah (thanks to royal permission from a new and benevolent Babylonian king), standing on the rubble of a city they had only heard about from their parents, and determined to rebuild. They are opposed, however, by the non-Jewish inhabitants of the area, who had gotten used to all the elbow room during the years since Judah had pretty much been emptied of its Jews.
THE PEOPLE	Zechariah, a prophet, is among the Jewish returnees. Zerubbabel is the general contractor for the Rebuild Jerusalem project (see Ezra 3:8).
WHAT ZECHARIAH'S WHOLE BOOK IS GENERALLY ABOUT	The prophet records several bizarre symbols that an angel showed him—symbols that warn and encourage the men and women who are clearing away the 70-year-old rubble of Jerusalem and the temple to rebuild them. The point of the symbols is simple: You've come home! You can rest now! Time to rebuild, especially the Temple! God has made your fasts into feasts! Peace is just around the corner!
A WORD ABOUT OIL	Oil—olive oil, to be exact—is widely believed to represent the Holy Spirit of God. And lamps burned olive oil.

• **Verse 6 contains the focus** of this passage: "This is the word of the Lord to Zerubbabel: 'Not by might nor by power, but by my Spirit,' says the Lord Almighty."

• **The might and power God is talking about here** is usually thought to be *human effort*. Yet if that's true—if God's work is to be done by his Spirit, not by human effort—what is God getting at? Obviously, Zerubbabel and his teams of laborers and craftsmen were doing a *lot* of lifting, building, and sweating in reconstructing the temple (see verse 9). Even today, church leaders and religious speakers are always encouraging you to stop trying to do things your way and, instead, let God do things in your life *his* way. How does this work in real life?

• **Check out verse 7,** about moving a mountain. What mountain did Zerubbabel have to move? What in your life once seemed as impossible to change as moving a mountain—yet somehow, against all hope, it happened? What seemingly impossible mountains are in your way now?

• **Speaking of moving mountains...**does this remind you of anything Jesus said half a millennium later about mountains, faith, and mustard seeds? Check it out in Matthew 17:20, then talk about this statement by Jesus. What do you think Jesus meant, especially by the last sentence in verse 20? Did he intend to be taken literally or figuratively? Talk about this.

• **Look at verse 10:** "Who despises the day of small things?" is a rhetorical question—you know, a question with an obvious answer, a question asked not to get an answer but to make a point. Like a parent whose 15-year-old asks if he can take a road trip to Orlando with a friend, and who replies, "Do I look stupid?" She's not innocently asking for her son's opinion of her I.Q.—she's making a point: "I'm not stupid, and you're taking no road trip." (Parents can be soooo narrow minded.)

Zechariah's point is equally clear: *Don't despise the day of small things,* he says. *The day the last of this rubble is cleared away and Zerubbabel gets out his level and plumb line and actually starts building—this will be a huge milestone!*

Name one of your recent "days of small things"— when something that looked small but was actually highly significant or influential happened to you or to someone close to you.

Bottom line

However you cut it, "it is God who works in you to will and to act according to his good purpose," as St. Paul put it to the Macedonian Christians in the city of Philippi (2:13). Whatever good behavior we're able to muster up now and then doesn't get us God's grace, but is somehow our response to grace—which comes to us freely, no strings attached, not because we deserve it, but because we need it.

[1]Then the angel who talked with me returned and wakened me, as a man is wakened from his sleep. [2]He asked me, "What do you see?" I answered, "I see a solid gold lampstand with a bowl at the top and seven lights on it with seven channels to the lights. [3]Also there are two olive trees by it, one on the right of the bowl and the other on the left." [4]I asked the angel who talked with me, "What are these, my lord?" [5]He answered, "Do you not know what these are?" "No, my Lord," I replied. [6]So he said to me, "This is the word of the Lord to Zerubbabel: 'Not by might nor by power, but by my Spirit,' says the Lord Almighty. [7]"What are you, O mighty mountain? Before Zerubbabel you will become level ground. Then he will bring out the capstone to shouts of 'God bless it! God bless it!'" [8]Then the words of the Lord came to me: [9]"The hands of Zerubbabel have laid the foundation of this temple; his hands will also complete it. Then you will know that the Lord Almighty has sent me to you. [10]"Who despises the day of small things? Men will rejoice when they see the plumb line in the hand of Zerubbabel. "(These seven are the eyes of the Lord, which range throughout the earth.)"

—Zechariah 4:1-10

*"For it is by grace you have been saved...
not by works, so that no one can boast."*

Read Ephesians chapter 2—yes, all 22 verses without stopping. You can linger over the details later. For now, just read it like you would a letter. And what a coincidence—it *is* a letter!

[1]As for you, you were dead in your transgressions and sins, [2]in which you used to live when you followed the ways of this world and of the ruler of the kingdom of the air, the spirit who is now at work in those who are disobedient. [3]All of us also lived among them at one time, gratifying the cravings of our sinful nature and following its desires and thoughts. Like the rest, we were by nature objects of wrath.
[4]But because of his great love for us, God, who is rich in mercy, [5]made us alive with Christ even when we were dead in transgressions—it is by grace you have been saved. [6]And God raised us up with Christ and seated us with him in the heavenly realms in Christ Jesus, [7]in order that in the coming ages he might show the incomparable richness of his grace, expressed in his kindness to us in Christ Jesus. [8]For it is by grace you have been saved, though faith—and this not from yourselves, it is the gift of God—[9]not by works, so that no one can boast. [10]For we are God's workmanship created in Christ Jesus to do good works, which God prepared in advance for us to do.
[11]Therefore, remember that formerly you who are Gentiles by birth and called "uncircumcised" by those who call themselves "the circumcision" (that done in the body by the hands of men)—[12]remember that at that time you were separate from Christ, excluded from citizenship in Israel and foreigners to the covenants of the promise, without hope and without God in the world. [13]But now in Christ Jesus you who were once far away have been brought near through the blood of Christ.
[14]For he himself is our peace, who has made the barrier, the dividing wall of hostility, [15]by abolishing in his flesh the law with its commandments and regulations. His purpose was to create in himself one new man out of the two, thus making peace, [16]and in this one body to reconcile both of them to God through the cross, by which he put to death their hostility. [17]He came and preached peace to you who were far away and peace to those who were near. [18]For through him we both have access to the Father by one Spirit.
[19]Consequently, you are no longer foreigners and aliens, but fellow citizens with God's people and members of God's household, [20]built on the foundation of the apostles and prophets, whit Christ Jesus himself as the chief cornerstone. [21]In him the whole building is joined together and rises to become a holy temple in the Lord. [22]And in him you too are being built together to become a dwelling in which God lives by his Spirit.

—Ephesians 2

- **St. Paul's thoughts** in this passage seem to flow something like this:

   ~ How the Ephesians lived *before* they became Christians (verses 1-3)

   ~ How and why grace came to them (4-10)

   ~ How the Ephesians, being Gentiles (i.e., non-Jews) and consequently uncircumcised, had formerly had no part in Israel's most-favored-nation status (11-12)

   ~ What Jesus did to that circumcision barrier that kept Gentiles apart from God (14-18)

   ~ Now, one big happy family: Gentiles as well as Jews, brought together in Christ (19-22)

- **Verses 8-9 seems to sum up** what Paul is pounding away at in this letter: "For it is by grace you have been saved, through faith-and this not from yourselves, it is the gift of God—not by works, so that no one can boast."

- **This chapter is crammed with Christology**—yes, you're right: theology about Christ. How many specific, direct Christ-things can you find—deeds he has done, traits of his, whatever?

- **About verses 1-3...do you think** the apostle is describing just the Ephesians before they became Christians? Or is he describing *everyone's* pre-Christian experience? Or do you think some parts of this passage are specific to the Ephesians, and other parts are universally true? Which, if any, parts of these verses remind you of your own pre-Christian days? If you're not a Christian, how accurately do you believe this describes you now?

- **What Paul wrote in verse 15** is nothing less than explosive, about Jesus "abolishing in his flesh the law with its commandments and regulations." Apparently what God gives—like the Mosaic law—God also can take away. And without the law there was no more division of all people into Jews ("those who were near") and non-Jews ("those who were far away").
   Nothing could be more scandalous to legalists.
   So what's the upshot? According to **Paul's words in verse 19**, what are the Gentile converts *no longer*? What have the Gentile converts become instead?

Talk about unearned grace

• We may not have circumcision anymore, but—in spite of what we say about grace—what rites, practices, or behaviors do we tend to require before we believe someone's salvation?

• Rate how deeply you *really* believe that grace alone is responsible for a person's salvation. Make your mark wherever on the line best represents your belief.

●——●

There are some serious obligations on the part of anyone who wants to be called by Christ's name.

Sure, grace is pretty much free, but at the same time you just can't waltz into it like you own it or something.

Grace is absolutely, utterly free to everyone. If a person can deserve grace, then it isn't grace.

• It's easy for us humans to let admiration for a religious person stretch into believing that person is downright holy. What is it about such people that encourages this? What do they have or do that seems to invite us to make saints of them? [size of congregations in megachurches, TV or radio show, SRO performances by Christian bands, sacrificial existence in Third World or among tribal people, monastics. i.e., the conspicuous on both ends]

• What people or kinds of people do you tend to believe are "far away" from God like uncircumcised non-Jews, who, as St. Paul wrote, were once far away from God? Who aren't on God's most-favored-people list? Atheists? Muslims? TV evangelists? Buddhists? Pornographers? Lawyers? White supremacists? Anyone in Hollywood?

By his decision

In this resource cluster:
- A primer on the doctrine of election...plus teaching points *(Will and Grace)*
- Bible study about God choosing us; various New Testament verses *(Who's in Charge Here, Anyway?)*
- Discussion-starting Qs *(Talk about who chose whom)*

teaching points

Since the beginning of time, people have pondered whether we choose our own paths in life from a grab-bag of opportunities or whether we're fated to make the decisions we do. Is life "Just do it" or "It was meant to be"? Or some combination of the two?

Don't be too quick to dismiss these ancient people as hopeless believers in magic. We may be modern, but we believe in magic all the same: we actually believe that honking our horns will clear a traffic jam.

How about our God? Does our Yahweh cause or does he allow?

Our salvation: did we choose God, or did he choose us?

Will and Grace

Go back into human history as far as you want, and you'll find that we have always been fussing with the question of why things happen. Why do we do what we do? Do we choose our own paths, or do deities set us on a course that is impossible to veer from? Are we puppets who merely act out a script the gods wrote, or that God wrote, or that fate compels us to follow? Or do our lives unfold not according to a plan, but according to a combination of deliberate choices, genes, and by being at the right place at the right time? Or does God call the shots, making it only *look* like we're choosing our way through life? Or do we actually choose our path through life, and God comes along for the ride?

That old Greek, Homer, wrote that Athena and Apollo were on the Plains of Troy right alongside the Greeks and the Trojans, invisibly aiding and abetting those warriors they favored, turning the tide of battle back and forth with their divine interference. The Israeli army was able to sack Jericho, the book of Joshua implies, because Yahweh himself tipped the city's walls over. Romeo and Juliet were destined to a short and unhappy romance because their horoscopic stars were misaligned. (The heavens' stars and planets have always been a popular explanation of why things happen.)

The Christian church started trying to answer these questions almost as soon as Christ left the scene. And theories have pendulumed back and forth ever since: God *causes* all stuff to happen, and we go along for the ride...God *lets* all things happen, though he knows beforehand what that stuff is...God *causes* good stuff to happen and *allows* bad stuff to happen...God will make everything to turn out all right in the end, but getting there is up to us and our decisions...we make things happen, and God goes along for the ride.

Of course, each of these theories sprouts from some idea in the Bible, and many start with this premise (roughly): If God is God, he certainly is in some kind of control of human events as they unfold. But exactly *how* God controls stuff and *to what degree* God controls stuff—well, here is where biblical clarity stops, and where everyone begins guessing. Pastor, bishop, seminary professor, TV preacher—they all have their own ideas about how it works.

Among the many aspects of this who-causes-stuff-to-happen debate is this: How responsible are humans for their salvation? Does God choose whom he wants to be saved, or do humans choose salvation for themselves? If God does the choosing, isn't he being a tad unfair to those he *doesn't* choose? And if we choose for ourselves, doesn't that diminish God's supposed all-powerfulness and sovereignty?

The Bible is not much help in solving this problem as definitively as we'd like. All we have are lots of verses about God choosing us, and lots of verses about us needing to choose God, and often the ideas and even the Bible passages overlap, and all anyone can conclude is that both perspectives are somehow true because we live in a fuzzy reality where causes and results seldom line up neatly (despite what a lot of Christian writers and speakers tell you), and trying to figure it all out gives one a headache. Or a degree in theology.

And all this just trying to figure out what the stark, black and white words of the Bible mean. "Whoever is thirsty, let him come," wrote St. John (Revelation 22:17), then along comes St. Paul, who stirs the pot by writing that God "chose us in him before the creation of the world" (Ephesians 1:4). Somehow, we are responsible for choosing God. We can choose for or against him. It's up to us. In retrospect, however, having chosen God, we look back over our shoulders and see that what looked for the world like our choosing God was actually just another link in the chain of events that God himself had set into motion a long time ago. And even *this* explanation is shallow and childish and naïve compared to the rich, incomprehensible mystery of it all.

However inexplicable this whole subject is, the feeling that St. Paul and the other letter writers leave you with is *gratitude*—what a privilege, they say, to have been chosen by Jehovah God to be his own adopted child and have the run of his household of faith. (In other places, of course, these same writers talk about the privilege of sharing this wealth with unbelievers and of doing all we can to bring them, too, into God's family.)

The lyrics in the Lost And Found song "H-O-L-Y" talk about God's side of the choosing thing: "Not by my choice, but by his choosing.... Not when I plan, but when the Spirit comes.... Not by my deeds, but by his doing.... Not by myself, but by his son.... Not by circumcision, but by his decision." Because we just need to remember that, sometimes, it's not all about us. It's all about God.

The Bible and our experiences speak plainly that, somehow, both are true.

Whoever is thirsty, let him come; and whoever wishes, let him take the free gift of the water of life. (Revelation 22:17)

For he chose us in him before the creation of the world to be holy and blameless in his sight. (Ephesians 1:4)

Gratitude for having been chosen by God.

Sometimes, our salvation is not all about us—it's all about God.

"For he chose us in him before the creation of the world...."

Not many people will disagree with you about the human side of choosing Jesus and becoming a Christ-follower: clearly, the choice is in our hands, to choose Christ or reject him.

Yet there is lots of debating about the God side of becoming a Christian. Does he really choose some for salvation and reject others? If he does, is it fair? How does his choosing us fit with our choosing him?

Lots of questions, and the answers are in short supply even for theologians. Following are some of the classic verses that emphasize God's side—how he chose us. A first rule of understanding any written work—the Bible, a poem, the Congressional Record, whatever—is this: if you want to understand a word or verse or page, read the surrounding context. In this case, you may want to read the several verses on either side of those listed below.

After reading the verses, talk about ones that catch your attention, that you particularly disagree with, that seem to answer something for you. You may want to jot down some insights you or your group comes up with, or something memorable that one of you may say.

- For many are invited, but few are chosen. (Matthew 22:14)

- You did not choose me, but I chose you and appointed you to go and bear fruit—fruit that will last. (John 15:16)

- For he chose us in him before the creation of the world to be holy and blameless in his sight. (Ephesians 1:4)

- But we ought always to thank God for you, brothers loved by the Lord, because from the beginning God chose you to be saved through the sanctifying work of the Spirit and through belief in the truth. (2 Thessalonians 2:13)

- Listen, my dear brothers: Has not God chosen those who are poor in the eyes of the world to be rich in faith and to inherit the kingdom he promised those who love him? (James 2:5)

• But you are a chosen people, a royal priesthood, a holy nation, a people belonging to God, that you may declare the praises of him who called you out of darkness into his wonderful light. (1 Peter 2:9)

• They will make war against the Lamb, but the Lamb will overcome them because he is Lord of lords and King of kings—and with him will be his called, chosen and faithful followers. (Revelation 17:14)

Talk about who chose whom

• FREE—as in "Grace is free!"—sounds like the deal of a lifetime (and beyond, of course). Who doesn't fantasize about free cars, free homes, free Caribbean vacations, free college scholarships? But FREE also implies that you don't have nearly the control you think you do, or you'd like. FREE means it's out of your hands. In a word, FREE = powerlessness. You're at the mercy and whim of, and in the debt of, the giver.

So what might even free grace cost you after all? Have you experienced any of that cost yet? What did it look like? How did it feel? Any second thoughts about having accepted that free grace in the first place?

• One thing St. Paul and the other New Testament letter writers leave Christians feeling is pure gratitude for having been chosen. If you are a Christian, talk about how *you* feel having been chosen by God for eternal life. What do you guess would be the similarity or difference between the gratitude of an adult who virtually grew up Christian and the gratitude of someone who became a Christian as an adult?

• You may have heard the conviction that says (in so many words) that as long as even just one person in the world goes to bed hungry—or poor, or illiterate, or dying from a curable disease, etc.—we have no right to feel comfortable ourselves.

In what ways does this conviction seem valid to you? In what ways does it seem unrealistic to you? How do you deal with the reality of being in the world's top 10 percent economically? (i.e., what you yourself spend—or what is spent on many U.S. high schoolers—in two or three months is the *annual household income* for billions of people in the world.)

Now shift this idea into the spiritual: how easy is it for you to be grateful for the free gift of grace while knowing that friends or family members or classmates or teammates do *not* have this gift? Does the Bible offer any help at reconciling this tension?

• If you're a Christian, how much of your becoming a Christian felt like your choice and how much felt like God pursued and chose you? Make your mark wherever on the line best represents your feelings.

●━━━━━━━━━━━━━━━━━━━━━━━━━━━━━━━━━━━━━━●

GOD CHOSE ME
I sure wasn't looking for God when he chose me for salvation.
OR
God reached down and pulled me kicking and screaming into his kingdom. (Once I was in, of course, I stopped kicking and screaming. Mostly.)

A BIT OF BOTH
I was clearly the one who made the decision to become a Christian. But in retrospect, I now recognize signs that God was pursuing me, leading me right up to my decision.

I CHOSE GOD
I've wanted God ever since I can remember. When it came to a decision, I jumped at the chance to become a Christian.

BLSQD

1. So free yet so enslaved.
So desperate yet so saved.
So dead, so risen from the grave.

2. So chasing yet so chased.
So permanent and so erased.
So repeated, so replaced.

3. So lost and yet so found.
In the sky and on the ground.
So dumb, so full of sound.

4. So sick and yet so cured.
So cool, such a nerd.
Brought together and divided by the Word.

5. So indebted so redeemed.
So dirty, yet so clean.
So dependent and so weaned.

6. Sometimes wolves and sometimes sheep.
So surface yet so deep.
So much to lose, so much to keep.

Mary the Convert

Rent the video of the Franco Zeffirelli TV miniseries *Jesus of Nazareth* (1977) and show the clip depicting the Annunciation: the angel Gabriel's announcement to the virgin Mary (Olivia Hussey) that she is to be the virgin mother of Jesus.

Although this isn't a sin-to-salvation conversion for Mary, all the traditional marks of conversion are here: astonishment, surrender, the realization that her life is forever changed. And during this moment the audience hears not a word from Gabriel, only the light that pours into the room—a touch that, the more you think about it, is probably as biblical as it is realistic.

First read together the biblical account of the Annunciation in Luke 1:26-40. Then introduce the clip with words to this effect:

> *Jesus of Nazareth clip*
> • **Reset counter** when "Sir Lew Grade presents" appears on screen
> • **Start clip: about 00:08:34**—when the officiating priest joins the hands of Mary and Joseph and says, "May this betrothal one to the other..."
> • **Stop clip: about 00:12:46**—when Mary says to her mother, "...she's going to have a son, and I must go and visit her."

> *Here is one director's interpretation of the Annunciation, when the angel Gabriel announced to Mary that she would become the mother of Jesus. This is kind of a conversion for Mary—not the kind of sin-to-salvation conversion we usually think of when we hear the word, but it certainly turned her world upside down like a conversion does: it dropped her to her knees (as you'll see), it was something she surrendered to.*

Then show the clip. Afterwards take five minutes to get the kids' reaction to Zeffirelli's cinematic interpretation of the Annunciation.

Bonus musing:

In Zeffirelli's mother-daughter dialogue that you saw, what small detail of Gabriel's news did Mary *not* tell her mother? Why do you feel that Mary held back? Why do you suppose she wanted to confide in her aunt Elizabeth rather than in her own mother? Ever feel like that yourself?

The Grace of Conversion

In this resource cluster:
• Where we got our image of conversion...some modern conversion stories (C.S. Lewis, Frederick Buechner, John Wesley, Ann Lamott, M. Scott Peck)...plus teaching points *(A Conversion Sampler)*
• A Bible study about two apparently very different conversions—Paul and his protégé, Timothy: Acts 9 and 2 Timothy 1:5 *(Mysteries of Conversion)*
• Discussion-starting Qs *(Talk about the mystery of your conversion)*

teaching points

A Conversion Sampler

Whatever it is you think you know, give it up. There are powers at play in the world about which you know very little.
[David Whyte, *Crossing the Unknown Sea*]

Where we get our popular image of conversion

• the conversion of Saul of Tarsus (Acts 9)

Our ideal of Christian conversion owes most of its imagery to the many tellings of St. Paul's conversion (Acts 9) when he was still Saul of Tarsus, a fiercely zealous Pharisee bent on keeping Judaism pure...the Jerusalem bounty hunter on the road with an arrest warrant in his hand for heretic Christians in Damascus. He was interrupted enroute to his mission, however, by the same Jesus whose followers he was out to get. Knocked off his feet and blinded by a flash of light, he immediately knew with whom it was he was dealing, and became instantly compliant.

• the conversion of the Philippian jailer (Acts 16)

Or the jailer in the prisons of Philippi (Acts 16), who within minutes goes from content pagan to desperate searcher to grateful Christian, thanks to a career-threatening earthquake and the providential presence of St. Paul among the prisoners.

Conversion as an instant U-turn (Toyota)

"Once I was blind, but now I see," go the lyrics to at least one gospel song. Dark—light, off—on, lost—saved. The spiritual U-turn of conversion is popularly represented—and often experienced—as a Toyota would make it: a quick one-eighty in an intersection, and two seconds later accelerating in the opposite direction.

Conversion as a gradual process (the turning of an oil tanker)

Such conversions are visible, measurable, and gratifying. Yet many experience conversion like an ocean-going oil tanker whose bulk requires miles to turn around. And when you're aboard such vessels as they turn, it is not always obvious that you *are* turning—the ship is huge, and there are few if any points of reference at sea by which to gauge the rate of your turn. Until, that is, the turn is almost completed, and you realized by unmistakable signs that you're headed in the opposite direction now.

Conversions look different on different converts...as on these modern converts:

Conversions are of all types. Any one conversion, in fact, contains both immediate and gradual elements. For proof of this, consider the following handful of conversions of writers, most of who, after their conversions, wrote (some are still writing) about faith for unchurched and unbelieving readers.

• C.S. Lewis...

Raised by a High Church father and tutored by a satirical atheist, **C.S. Lewis** returned home to England from the front lines of World War I wounded, and after recovering finished his studies and became a fellow and tutor of literature

...an atheist, took a decade to pare down the intellectual options until he was left with Christianity as the only viable explanation of things...

at Oxford. Over the next decade his defenses against a supernatural, monotheistic, grace-filled Christianity evaporated one by one, until he was left looking at Christianity as the only plausible and logical explanation of things. Finally, after a long, late-night walk with a friend, he realized that

> That which I greatly feared had at last come upon me. In the Trinity Term of 1929 I gave in, and admitted that God was God, and knelt and prayed: perhaps, that night, the most dejected and reluctant convert in all England. I did not then see what is now the most shining and obvious thing; the Divine humility which will accept a convert even on such terms. (*Surprised by Joy*)

...he went on to write The Lion, the Witch, and the Wardrobe (among the other Chronicles of Narnia).

Lewis, of course, is the author of (among many titles) *The Chronicles of Narnia*, *Mere Christianity*, *The Screwtape Letters*, and the sci-fi/fantasy Space Trilogy. Even before his death in 1963, he was acclaimed as Christianity's greatest apologist of the 20th century.

• John Wesley...

...ordained minister in the Church of England...

...missionary to colonial Georgia in America...

...lasted less than two years before returning home to England...

...realized his spiritual poverty, that something was missing...

Another Englishman, **John Wesley**, was born into the large and devoutly Anglican Wesley family. Having set his sights early on the church as a calling, and having received a thorough religious training, he was ordained a clergyman in the Church of England, and in 1736 became a missionary to the American colony of Georgia.

He did not survive even two years there. His legalistic, by-the-book approach to ministry wasn't appreciated by his parishioners. It all hit the fan when he fell in love with and planned to marry the attractive daughter of an official. For some reason the engagement was broken, she quickly married another, and John Wesley—in a combination of legalism, hurt feelings, and spite—refused to serve communion to his ex-fiancée and parishioner. A lawsuit ensued, and he soon found himself on a boat headed back to England.

He was miserable and, even though a minister, full of doubts about his own spiritual standing. "I went to America to convert the Indians," Wesley wrote in his journal, "but, O! who shall convert me? who, what is he that will deliver me from this evil heart of unbelief?" He found his answer a few months after returning home. On a May evening he reluctantly attended a little meeting on Aldersgate Street in London, where a handful of Christians met in a society for prayer and Bible study. It was while someone was reading aloud Martin Luther's preface to the New Testament book of Romans—about saving faith— that Wesley was forever changed:

...on Aldersgate Street, finally felt his heart "strangely warmed" with the assurance of his salvation...

> About a quarter before nine, while he was describing the change which God works in the heart through faith in Christ, I felt my heart strangely warmed. I felt I did trust in Christ, Christ alone, for salvation; and an assurance was given me that he had taken away my sins, even mine, and saved me from the law of sin and death. (*Journals and Diaries*)

Although he had been intellectually intimate with Jesus for a long time, it was Wesley's heart that was finally affected that night on Aldersgate. He soon acquired a reputation for taking holy communion to the miners and other labor-

... and became the founder
of Methodism.

ers where they worked and lived, instead of requiring them to attend a sometimes distant church. And, of course, he is the father of Methodism.

• M. Scott Peck, author of
The Road Less Traveled...

The psychiatrist **M. Scott Peck**, author of the best-selling *The Road Less
Traveled: A New Psychology of Love, Traditional Values and Spiritual Growth*,
talked about his conversion in a *Door* interview (May/June 1990):

...a non-Christian, yet invited
by some insightful nuns to
take communion with them
regularly...

> The reason I became a Christian is that I fell in with this fast group of
> nuns three or four years before I was baptized, and they accepted me
> into their community and allowed me to take communion with them.
> The Mother Superior said she had written the bishop and received a dis-
> pensation for me [since Roman Catholicism, like many Christian faiths
> and denominations, require baptism into that faith or church before par-
> ticipation in communion is permitted], but I don't think she ever asked
> him. I celebrated the Eucharist quite intensively before I became bap-
> tized.

...and this community became
the eventual means of his
conversion to Christianity.

Participation in this sacrament, officially reserved for practicing
Christians in many churches, became for Peck the gradual *means* of grace and
his conversion, as he regularly took this spiritual meal with these women of
faith.

• Frederick Buechner...

...not a churchgoer, yet wan-
dered into the church next
door on an impulse...

...and listened to a forgettable
sermon, except for the last
part—specifically, one
phrase: that Jesus is crowned
in our hearts with "great
laughter."

Frederick Buechner was 27, living alone in New York City, in love with a girl who
did not love him, and trying unsuccessfully to write a book. On a Sunday
morning he attended the church next door—on impulse only, since he was not
a churchgoer.

He wrote later that the only part of the sermon he remembered clearly
was the last part, in which the preacher compared the coronation of Jesus to
the coronation of Elizabeth II, an event all over the news in 1953:

> He said that unlike Elizabeth's coronation in the Abbey, this coronation
> of Jesus in the believer's heart took place among confession—and I
> thought, yes, yes, confession—and tears, he said—and I thought tears,
> yes, perfectly plausible that the coronation of Jesus in the believing
> heart should take place among confession and tears. And then...he said
> in his odd, sandy voice...that the coronation of Jesus took place among
> confession and tears and then, as God was and is my witness, *great
> laughter*, he said. Jesus is crowned among confession and tears and
> great laughter, and at the phrase *great laughter*, for reasons that I have
> never satisfactorily understood, the great wall of China crumbled and
> Atlantis rose up out of the sea, and on Madison Avenue, at 73rd Street,
> tears leapt from my eyes as though I had been struck across the face.
> (*The Alphabet of Grace*)

And that ordinary, mundane
phrase undid him, and was the
means of his conversion.

Following his conversion Buechner attended seminary, became an
ordained Presbyterian minister, and again found his writing voice. Among his
several novels is *Godric*, which was nominated for the Pulitzer Prize. His nonfic-
tion, meanwhile—*Wishful Thinking: A Theological ABC* and *Telling the Truth: the
Gospel as Tragedy, Comedy, and Fairy Tale*, among many others—strikes many

readers as a primer for the unchurched, writing as he does outside the typical Christianese and Godtalk. Instead he relates Bible people and events in gritty, mundane, everyday language—which makes those of us who inhabit the gritty, mundane, everyday world think that, just maybe, the God of the Bible can be our God, too.

Anne Lamott remembers, "my coming to faith did not start with a leap but rather a series of staggers from what seemed like one safe place to another."

The safe places were few and far between. Growing up in an affluent family outside San Francisco during the '70s, in high school she began gravitating to wherever the dope and alcohol were. In a college class one day, a favorite teacher read Kierkegaard aloud, a passage in which he retells the story of Abraham's intended sacrifice of his son Isaac.

"In the interior silence that followed my understanding of this scene," Lamott writes in *Traveling Mercies*, "I held my breath for as long as I could, sitting there under the fluorescent lights—and then I crossed over. I don't know how else to put it or how and why I actively made, if not exactly a *leap* of faith, a lurch of faith.... I left class believing—accepting—that there was a God."

Fast-forward through a decade of alcoholism and desperate feelings of losing herself and writing and selling some books. Lamott was curled up on her bed in the dark, bleeding heavily from an abortion, drunk and stoned—and suddenly conscious beyond all doubt of Jesus in the room with her: "I felt him just sitting there on his haunches in the corner of my sleeping loft, watching me with patience and love, and I squinched my eyes shut, but that didn't help because that's not what I was seeing him with."

A week later she went to a ramshackle little church she had discovered earlier and attended occasionally, and actually stayed through the sermon this time, but it was hearing the tiny congregation sing the closing hymn that undid her: "I felt like their voices or *something* was holding me like a scared kid, and I opened up to that feeling—and it washed over me."

She started to cry, left before the benediction, walked to her house and in the front door, stood there a minute, and said, "I quit. All right. You can come in."

Add to these stories *your* conversion. Was it like Lewis', a gradual elimination of options until you were left looking at Christianity not as the best option, but the *only* option? Or like Lamott, were you relentlessly trailed by God on little cat feet for years as you dug yourself deeper into your own despair, until finally you just gave up, gave in, and said yes? Or did you do things all backwards—like Wesley, becoming a true Christian only *after* you had been in ministry for years? Or like Peck, doing Christian things as a means of becoming a Christian, rather than a result of it?

The point, of course, is that people come to faith, to Jesus, to salvation for all sorts of reasons and in all sorts of ways. And as long as you end up in Jesus, they're all good. Some get more publicity than others...some are more visible or measurable...but they're all good. However it happened, whether in tears or in laughter, your eyes finally saw, your heart softened, you said yes to Jesus in a way you hadn't ever before.

"He fell to the ground and heard a voice"

Read Acts 9

• The Acts passage narrates the conversion of Saul of Tarsus, known shortly thereafter as Paul.

• Paul's conversion was a knock-down, drag-out affair: he was knocked down by the presence of Jesus on the road to Damascus, so that as a Christian witness for Jesus he could be beaten and dragged out of cities. Okay, bad pun, but nonetheless true: read verses 15-16. (For fulfillment of this divine purpose, see Acts 14:19.)

> I have been reminded of your sincere faith, which first lived in your grandmother Lois and in your mother Eunice and, I am persuaded, now lives in you also. —2 Timothy 1:5

• Where in this chapter can you find hard evidence of Saul's pre-conversion attitude toward Jesus and his followers? What do the following Bible verses tell you about this?
> ~ Acts 7:54 - 8:1
> ~ Acts 26:9-11
> ~ Philippians 3:4-7 (especially verse 6)

• What evidence is there in this chapter that Saul experienced some instantaneous changes? That he went from Christ hater to Christ lover pretty quickly?

• Some Christians talk about a "Damascus road" conversion. What do you think they mean?

Read 2 Timothy 1:5

• This is the only biblical clue we have about the conversion of Paul's young protégé Timothy.

• With a devoutly Christian mother and grandmother, what might you guess were the circumstances of Timothy's conversion? How does this image compare to Saul's conversion?

• What are some differences that you can imagine (or that you've observed) between childhood conversions and adult conversions?

Finally...

• Anything in any of these verses that's a puzzle to you? That just doesn't make sense?

• What one thing got your attention most of all in these verses? Why did it affect you like it did?

Bonus study for those itching for a little controversy

Paul was arrested in Jerusalem for inciting a riot and for religious desecration (Acts 24:5-7). Acts 26 recounts Paul's defense before Agrippa, a local king. In his defense Paul retells the circumstances of his Damascus-road conversion.

What are the similarities between this account and the Acts 9 account? What are the differences? Use this chart if it helps:

So What Really *Did* Happen, Anyway?
Comparison of two accounts of Paul's conversion: Acts 9 and 26

<u>Similarities</u>	<u>Differences</u>

• So...what about those differences? Can you account for them?

• Do they matter?

• The book of Acts bears Luke's name as author. What do these differences say about his credibility? Or look at it another way: what does Luke's letting two variations of Saul's conversion *stand* tell you about the writer's credibility?

Talk about the mystery of your conversion

• If you have experienced Christian conversion, which (if any) of the 5 people whose conversion stories you've heard about most resembles yours?

• Which is most dissimilar to yours?

• Make your mark wherever along the line best represents your feelings.

●━━━●

My Christian conversion was a very emotional thing.   My Christian conversion was a very intellectual thing.

Talk among yourselves about why you marked where you did.

• It is common for people saved one way to wonder about what it would have been like to have been saved *another* way. The Christian who grows up in a Christian home and cannot remember ever *not* being a Christian wonders if Christianity would be more meaningful if she had been saved in her thirties. And the Christian who was saved in his thirties imagines how much easier his life would have been if he had grown up in a Christian home as a child.

     Have you ever felt this way? What have you observed about those two kinds of Christians? Talk about this.

• Make your mark wherever along the line best represents your feelings.

●━━━●

I am perfectly content with the circumstances and timing of my conversion to Christ. No regrets.

Sometimes I wonder if this or that in my life would have happened if I had been converted sooner or later than I was. But God knew the best time, regardless of how I feel about it.

I can get almost mad about the timing of my Christian conversion. I mean, I'm forever grateful for it—but I would've been spared so much grief if I had come to Christ at a different point in my life.

Talk among yourselves about why you marked where you did.

• The popular image of conversion is a before-and-after thing—that is, conversion (to Christ, to veganism, to the GOP, whatever) happens once, it is a one-time turning around, and it forever changes your life. Others say that life is a series of conversions, many milestones along the way—some of course more memorable or life-shifting than others, but in any case not limited to just One Big Event.

     What do you think? What have you experienced? What have you observed or read of the experience of others? Talk about this.

• If you have not experienced Christian conversion, why not?

• If you became a Christian recently, why did you not become one earlier?

Writers' option

Put in writing the story of your conversion—the lead-up (minutes or years), the circumstances of the moment (if it was a moment, which it may not have been), and the immediate aftermath. Sometimes it's easier to get flowing if you picture someone you're writing to, so decide who you can trust with the information you want to write, and imagine this friend or relative as you write.

BABY

1. Her shaved head and her pierced nose
Her big rottweilers and her tie-dyed clothes
Her Doctor Martens and her biker tights
Her long, black leggings on a hot summer night.

chorus
    And nobody calls her baby,
    Nobody says "I love you so."
    Nobody calls her baby,
    Oh I guess she'll never know.

2. His working boots and flannel shirts
His sympathies buried as deep as his hurts
Long, lonely walks with nowhere to go
And his only appointment is with a TV show.

3. Eighty pounds she's hardly whole
Losing her body to gain some control
Hours alone in some tanning salon
Trying a smaller and smaller size on.

4. His pin-stripe suit and his wing-tip shoes
His laptop computer and his Wall Street News
he makes his plane and keeps his pace
He hides his pain behind a poker face.

ending chorus
But Somebody loves those babies
Somebody loves what we can't see.
And if somebody told them, maybe
Those babies would be free.

Baby Talk

For each clue below, the answer is a word that ends in the sound *bee*—such as in the word *baby*. Read the clues one at a time to your group, and let them respond. If your kids are gonzo-competitive, pit one team against another.

- striped cat   *[tabby]*

- monastery   *[abbey]*

- talkative   *[gabby]*

- influential special-interest group   *[lobby]*

- brand of canned vegetables   *[Libby]*

- stop-action claymation character like Mr. Bill   *[Gumby]*

- fatso   *[tubby]*

- hat or a horse race   *[derby]*

- male spouse   *[hubby]*

- F. Scott Fitzgerald character   *[Gatsby]*

- British field game...said to be part soccer, part American football, and part streetfighting
    [rugby]

- grouchy   *[crabby]*

- talking toy of the '90s   *[Furbie]*

- woman's last name in a Beatles song   *[Rigby]*

- relaxing pastime   *[hobby]*

- out of shape...lacking muscle tone   *[flabby]*

- UK cop   *[bobby]*

Baby Talk 2

Talk about the two common meanings of *baby*—helpless infant and sweetheart—as they appear in these common expressions:

• You big baby.

• Don't be such a baby.

• Hey baby, wanna dance?

• Don't cry, baby.

• Oh, he's such a beautiful baby!

• Be my, be my baby...oh no, don't say maybe....

• It's your turn to change the baby.

• "Baby, Baby" [*The ultimate crossover song by Amy Grant: when it was released, she claimed it was about her then-newborn infant—while the music video was replete with boyfriend-girlfriend images.*]

Talk about why the same word seems so appropriate for two so apparently different uses. Or are there more similarities between the two uses than first meet the eye?...

God wants you badly enough to chase you down

In this resource cluster:
• God is so deliberate about making sure we get the point of his grace, that he pursues us...plus teaching points *(We Are Wanted, Therefore We Are Chased)*
• A pair of Bible studies: Colossians 1:26-27 *(Being Jesus)* and Matthew 25:31-46 *(Whose Hands?)*
• Discussion-starting Qs *(Talk about the mysteries of being wanted, and of being Jesus)*

teaching points

We Are Wanted, Therefore We Are Chased

People are itchy and lost and bored and quick to jump at any fix. Why is there such a vast self-help industry in this country? Why do all these selves need help? They have been deprived of something by our psychological culture. They have been deprived of the sense that there is something else in life, some purpose that has come with them into the world.
[James Hillman, in an interview "From Little Acorns: A Radical New Psychology," *The Sun*, March 1998]

> Everybody wants—needs?—to be wanted.

Everyone wants to be loved, wants to be wanted, wants to be called baby in one sense or another, by someone or another. Animal families and packs have their brutal side—many species expel the weaned or the weak—yet among them are examples galore of unqualified acceptance, of community-wide nurturing of young, of instinctive and even sacrificial protection of their own from danger.

Too bad *homo sapiens* hasn't learned that lesson yet. With the gift of volition came the ability to make destructive decisions, and we seem bent on destroying ourselves and each other. Our species has to work hard, seemingly *against* instinct sometimes, to accept, to protect, and to cherish other individuals, whether within or outside of our families.

All of which hugely explains our need to be wanted and pursued by God, since not many of us have proven ourselves likely to go looking for him—despite our longings for unconditional acceptance as we are, for an eternal home, for some kind of meaning to life that was here before us and will remain after us.

> Part of what God's grace means is that he actively wants you and pursues you—just like he did—
>
> • Abraham

The hound of heaven

The poet Francis Thompson compared God to a hound on the hunt, who tenaciously keeps its nose on scent, who relentlessly tracks through muck and briar and darkness until it finally trees its quarry.

Abraham probably felt a little hounded, chased out of his comfortable condo in Ur by the foreign God Elohim, who did not permit him to settle for long even in far-off Haran, but insisted on chasing Abram to exactly where Elohim wanted him: smack-dab in the middle of Canaan. Even when Abram wasn't exactly impressed with that neighborhood and instead moved along to civilized Egypt—an urbanized land that reminded him of his native Ur—Elohim chased him back to Canaan.

- Jonah

- The Prodigal Son

God can use anyone to bring his grace to us.

God can use anything to bring his grace to us.

"God speaks to us through what happens to us—even through such unpromising events as walking up the road to get the mail out of the mailbox, maybe, or seeing something in the TV news that brings you up short, or laughing yourself silly with a friend. If skeptics ask to be shown an instance of God speaking to them in their lives, I suggest that they pay closer attention to the next time when, for unaccountable reasons, they find tears in their eyes."
—Frederick Buechner

Jonah, of course, is the classic biblical case of God not allowing someone to escape him. Sure, God had a job he wanted Jonah to do—but you get the idea that the Almighty saved Jonah from himself in the process, too.

And if the father of the Prodigal Son didn't actually track down the hedonistic boy and drag him back home, there's a feeling in the story that the father's *love* did just that somehow. How else could Dad have been waiting there at the property line for the boy to get sufficiently broke and return, first to his senses, then to home, where even the reek of pig manure didn't keep his father from hugging him?

We know we are loved by who chases us down, by who cares enough to come after us. That would be God, though there are no rules about who or what he can use to convince us of his love. Often it's other people. Think of the best things that you have ever done for someone: for that moment, you were a little Christ (isn't that what the word *Christian* means literally?), or the hands of God. Does God have any hands but yours when it comes down to changing a tire or a diaper for those who cannot do it themselves? If we depend upon God for life and breath and the mysteries of existence, then might not God depend upon us for all the gritty and mechanical mundanities of existence?

God uses not only other people to get our attention and draw us to him, but also events. Things. Stuff. Nothing is so bland or mundane or tedious that it cannot be used by God, especially in God's primary task of loving us to himself. You may know what this is like: you finish chores, you walk out of the barn and into the winter sunshine, and—as if the sun's warmth itself were the answer—you understand what has long been troubling you. Or in a season of personal anguish, you sit at a red light during your commute, and a bus flashes across your vision, and the words you glimpse in the banner ad on the bus side make you catch your breath, they are so personal. And the inexplicable comfort you feel from that day on, you are convinced, can be from nowhere or no one else but God.

In such mighty and mundane ways God convinces us of his loving grace, gathers us in his arms, calls us his babies, and cuddles us up, dirty diapers and all.

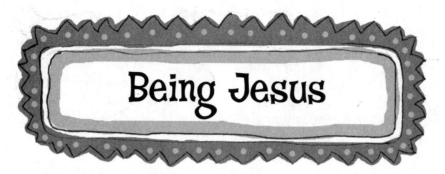

"Christ in you, the hope of glory."

Read Colossians 1:26-27.
You may want to jot down some insights you or your group come up with or something memorable that one of you may say.

• **When you read the word** *mystery* in the New Testament, it seems to refer to one (or more) of a few different things.

> 26...the mystery that has been kept hidden for ages and generations, but is now disclosed to the saints. 27To them God has chosen to make known among the Gentiles the glorious riches of this mystery, which is Christ in you, the hope of glory.

~ That Gentiles, not just Jews, can now know the grace of God (Romans 11:25-26; Romans 16:25-26; Ephesians 3:2-6; Ephesians 3:8-9)

~ How Christians, living and dead, will be taken to heaven at Christ's coming —popularly called the "rapture" (1 Corinthians 15:51 ff)

~ What God has prepared for those who love him (1 Corinthians 2:7-9)

~ The one-flesh union of husband and wife and its corresponding reality in the relationship between Christ and his church (Ephesians 5:32)

~ The Incarnation (Colossians 2:2-3; 1 Timothy 3:16)

~ The hidden meanings of various apocalyptic events and symbols (Revelations 1:20; Revelations 10:7; Revelations 17:5, 7)

• **Which of these meanings** do the Colossians 1 verses fit? Or is it yet another kind of mystery?

• **What does "Christ in you" mean to you?** What does it *not* mean to you? Talk about this.

Finally...

• Anything in these verses that's still a puzzle to you? That just doesn't make sense?

• What one thing got your attention most of all in these verses? Why did it affect you like it did?

Whose Hands?

"Whatever you did for one of the least of these brothers of mine, you did for me."

Read Matthew 25:31-46.
You may want to jot down some insights you or your group comes up with, or something memorable that one of you may say.

³¹When the Son of Man comes in his glory, and all the angels with him, he will sit on his throne in heavenly glory. ³²All the nations will be gathered before him, and he wills separate the people one from another as a shepherd separates the sheep from the goats. ³³He will put the sheep on his right hand and the goats on his left.
³⁴Then the King will say to those on his right, "Come, you who are blessed by my Father; take your inheritance, the kingdom prepared for you since the creation of the world. ³⁵For I was hungry and you gave me something to eat, I was thirsty and you gave me something to drink, I was a stranger and you invited me in, ³⁶I needed clothes and you clothed me, I was sick and you looked after me, I was in prison and you came to visit me."
³⁷Then the righteous will answer him, "Lord, when did we see you hungry and feed you, or thirsty and give you something to drink? ³⁸When did we see you a stranger and invite you in, or needing clothes and clothe you? ³⁹When did we see you sick or in prison and go to visit you?"
⁴⁰The King will reply, "I tell you the truth, whatever you did for the least of these brothers of mine, you did for me."
⁴¹Then he will say to those on his left, "Depart from me, you who are cursed, into the eternal fire prepared for the devil and his angels. ⁴²For I was hungry and you gave me nothing to eat, I was thirsty and you gave me nothing to drink, ⁴³I was a stranger and you did not invite me in, I was sick and in prison and you did not look after me."
⁴⁴They also will answer, "Lord, when did we see you hungry or thirsty or a stranger or needing clothes or sick or in prison, and did not help you?"
⁴⁵He will reply, "I tell you the truth, whatever you did not do for one of the least of these, you did not do for me."
⁴⁶Then they will go away to eternal punishment, but the righteous to eternal life.

—Matthew 25: 31-46

• **In the front yard of a church** in a tired, gritty neighborhood of Southeast San Diego is a larger-than-life statue of Jesus whose hands are lifted, palms up and perhaps waist high, as if showing passersby on the busy street the wounds on his hands. Except that he has no hands. His sculptured arms end bluntly at the wrists. A large, weathered sign at the base of the statue explains the anomaly: THE ONLY HANDS HE HAS ARE YOURS.

What are your feelings about a statue and a statement like this? Make your mark wherever along the line best represents your feelings.

●————————————————————————————————●

This is just a bizarre depiction of Jesus. I mean, what's it supposed to be, anyhow—Lord of the Stumps? This sort of thing only convinces people that Christians are wacko.

Sounds spiritual, but it's pretty much wrong. How can we who are sinful do the work of God? God may decide to use us now and then, but it's still *him* doing the work, and we're only tools in his hands— we're *not* his hands themselves.

An interesting point...but how does it work? What's the difference between *me* doing something, God doing something *through* me, and God just up and doing it on his own? Maybe in the end, it's all the same.

Right on. We're indispensable to God. If we don't do his work, it doesn't get done. He needs *us* to do it.

Talk about where on the line you marked, and why you marked there.

• Why are **those on the King's left—the "goats"**—turned away into eternal punishment, according to this passage?

• **How would you respond** to a friend who, after reading this passage, said this: "If it is true that we are saved by grace through faith and not by works, what business does God have sending some well-intentioned people to hell because they didn't do some good deeds?" Talk about this.

Finally...

• Anything in these verses that's still a puzzle to you? That just doesn't make sense?

• What one thing got your attention most of all in these verses? Why did it affect you like it did?

Talk about the mysteries of being wanted, and of being Jesus

• In what ways do people you know get others to appreciate or admire or love them?

• It's hard to imagine an Ally McBealized professional, sleek and sexy and well-paid and self-reliant, longing for someone to call her "Baby." Or is it?... Talk about this.

• Name some types of people you know who, at first glance or first thought, seem hardly the type who want to be wanted.

• Can you recall a time when another person was Jesus to you? If you can, and if it is appropriate, talk about the circumstances.

• Whom do you know well enough in your world to know that, in their own way, they want to be loved on by God? Is it possible that you could be Jesus to this person? What would this look like? Talk about this.

Kingdom

The Kingdom's big enough for you
You were made to be here too
The Kingdom's big enough for you
Where you are as you are

1. So many people pushed away
Ones that are loved told they can't stay
A question is what would Jesus say. Anyway...

2. But God's own people close the door
The loud and the angry take the floor
We see what you fear; but what are you for? Furthermore...

The Kingdom's big enough for you...

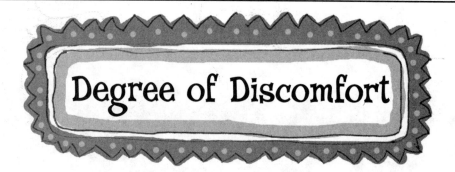

Degree of Discomfort

Query your students about the degree of discomfort they'd feel if these people walked into church and sat down next to them. Assume these people come to your church to worship, not to protest or make some sort of statement.

• the local director of Planned Parenthood
• local director of Christians Who Believe Abortion Is Murder
• a couple you know aren't married and living with each other
• a person you know is gay
• the only person who doesn't raise her hands in your church during worship
• the only person who raises his hands in your church during worship
• a congressional lobbyist for the Christian Coalition
• a convicted child molester, just released from prison and living in your church's neighborhood
• a known organizer for Legalize Marijuana Now Coalition

Time and interest permitting, you may also want to probe the reason for your students' discomfort (doctrinal? moral? political?). If you or your students cannot imagine such people attending your church, it may be worth probing the reasons for that, too.

Be Careful...or Else Just Anybody Will Walk In

The Visit

Read aloud to your kids part 1 of the Adrian Plass short story "The Visit" on pages 68-70. Set the scene for them before you start reading: the narrator is a church leader in present-day England—and Jesus is about to visit *his* world, *his* culture. And as you'll see, the narrator is at times close to shutting the door on even Jesus.

There is enough discussion potential in this excerpt to last your entire meeting, and probably the rest of the night. So read it first yourself, before the meeting, and decide how you want to use this reading.

Shut the Door!

In this resource cluster:
• How it is human nature to exclude...a snapshot of door-shutting Pharisaism, with a classic 20th-century example...plus teaching points (*Be Careful...or Else Just Anybody Will Walk In*)
• A Bible study: Matthew 23—the hypocrisies of the Pharisees (*Woe, Woe, Woe*)
• Discussion-starting Qs (*Talk about opening and closing doors*)

teaching points

You may want to illustrate this point with whatever [fill in the blank]–gate scandal is currently in the news—scandals involving politicians, businesspeople, clergy, entertainers. There is seldom a lack of this sort of thing.

You can shut a door for several reasons. To keep out a stink. To keep a room warm. To be private. To be cozy. To be illegal. To be quiet.

In our modern cultural climate, when a group (organization, association, company, church, etc.) shuts the door on people, the public almost always assumes it has something to hide. Of course, this is not necessarily true. Sometimes the group has nothing to hide, only certain people to keep out: People Not Like Us, or People We Don't Want In Here With Us, or People Who Are Not As [insert an adjective here—*polite, wealthy, patriotic, logical, creative, biblical,* etc.] As Us.

It seems part of human nature that when individuals with a common passion or interest begin to act as a group, exclusion is inevitably a step behind. Not that exclusion is inherently wrong. When you choose one thing, after all, you implicitly reject another thing. But too often the exclusion is the kind that shuts doors in faces, and keeps out those who have every right to be inside along with those in control.

It's especially ugly when doors are shut on people in the name of God. God, who is the source of all grace and forgiveness, seems to have got saddled with a wretched and undeserved reputation in this department. It goes to show that *no one* is safe from the lure of self-righteousness and control over others.

Which is exactly why Jesus roundly accused the leaders of that highly influential Jewish group of the first century, the Pharisees. "You shut the door of the kingdom of heaven in people's faces," Jesus told them in a scathing condemnation—and then proceeded to catalog their various hypocrisies.

In Matthew 23 Jesus catalogs the several kinds of hypocrisies of which the Pharisees were guilty—and most of them were related to shutting doors on people, keeping them out of what they themselves enjoyed.

I see a Pharisee
Two doors that the Pharisees shut in the face of the Jewish laity hold particular—and ominous—significance for us today.

Matthew 3:7-10

First, the Pharisees *shut the door on those whose interpretations of the Torah and its teachings differed from theirs.* "We have Abraham as our father," the Pharisees assured themselves, apparently not even for a moment imagining that Abraham could have more than one *type* of offspring. (St. Paul later fills out this picture, explaining that Abraham is the father of *all* who believe that God will actually do the impossible for them.) And when Jesus healed the blind and mute man of a demon, the Pharisees grabbed one conclusion and wouldn't let go of it: "It is only by Beelzebub, the prince of demons, that this fellow drives out demons."

"Understand, then, that those who believe are children of Abraham." (Galatians 3:7)

Matthew 12:22-29

Jesus, of course, couldn't let such a goofy lapse of logic stand, and annihilated it in a few succinct sentences.

Second, the Pharisees *shut the door on people who they feared could taint them morally.* Who you associated with was a big thing to Pharisees—especially entering the house of a "sinner," or (Yahweh forbid!) eating a meal with one.

Luke 15:1-2

In short, check out John 9:13-34 for a snapshot of Pharisaism at its worst:

In the John 9 incident, the Pharisees interrogated a man Jesus healed of blindness and ended up throwing him out.

• Immovable belief in their own doctrine and interpretations, even in the face of obvious evidence to the contrary;
• Use of authority by spiritual leaders to intimidate followers into acquiescence;
• Angry, accusative, defensive responses to simple statements of reality that undermine the rock wall of their authority.

Any of this feel familiar? Every generation has its own spiritual door shutters, its own variety of Pharisees who are determined to hold on to the creeds passed on to them even in the face of Jesus working among them—who are determined to measure spirituality in themselves and in their followers so that the righteous can be distinguished and separated from the unrighteous. Having identified themselves as righteous, they believe they maintain their spirituality by where they eat, with whom they eat, and what they eat—rather than by what comes out of their heart.

Every generation of Christians has its equivalent of pharisaical door shutting...

Let us consider an example that is safely in the past, so as not to bring any comparisons too close to home. Billy Graham had barely started shaving, and his citywide evangelistic revivals were picking up steam. His campaign team was discovering that they could drop into town, conduct a week or two of nightly meetings, and leave town hoping that the hundreds of converts they left behind would find their way into a church or somehow muddle along themselves into some kind of spiritual growth. Or the Graham team could meet with a town's clergy prior to the evangelistic meetings, engage the volunteer help within their congregations, and, when the Graham team left town at the end of the campaign, they'd be leaving converts in the care of the city's several churches.

...even during the 1950s: the Billy Graham Crusades.

The strength of Billy Graham's ministry was its having chosen the second route, of deliberately connecting new Christians with local churches so that new converts wouldn't fizzle in isolation when the evangelistic campaign folded its tents and left town.

Graham opened doors.

This strategy entailed, of course, meeting with a city's clergymen—as many as Graham could attract. And in the early 1950s, that was just about all of them. Evangelicalism hadn't acquired yet the kind of political and social conservatism that now alienates most mainline denominations; plus anything in the '50s remotely resembling Christianity that could attract as much attention as Graham could was welcomed with open arms by most Protestant leaders (and eventually Roman Catholic, too).

This is readily documented in any Graham biography, in any published study of the Billy Graham Crusades in the '50s, and in any text by or about Fundamentalists during this era.

So an assortment of clergymen—Methodist, Lutheran, Baptist, you name it—sat on the platform behind Graham's pulpit during the meetings. And this, believe it or not, became a prime reason why Fundamental churches tended to boycott the evangelistic meetings and trash Graham in general: not because the Fundamentalists disagreed with what Graham believed or what he preached, but because clergymen the Fundamentalists *didn't* agree with were up on the platform along with Graham.

Sin by association

Sin by association. And so not because of any doctrinal disagreement with Graham but merely because he *associated*—shared a platform—with mainline denominational clergy who were purveyors of liberal theology and, therefore, (supposedly) faux Christians and unscriptural reprobates, etc., etc.—because of this, Fundamentalists pretty much shut the door on any evangelistic efforts that involved cooperating with anyone whose doctrine wasn't as sanitary as theirs. Even if the goal of the cooperation was evangelism, with which Fundamentalists agree with their whole hearts.

Fundamentalists have no monopoly on Pharisaism. Chances are, a church you've worshiped or worked in has done its own share of door shutting. No doubt the church leaders have their reasons for shutting doors on people—and the reasons are always "biblical" or "scriptural" and usually done in the name of holiness or obedience to God. And no wonder they shut doors—to keep the door open usually means a messy, complicated affair that is difficult to manage. Would you do any differently?

You can go online and find no end of this sort of thing. Just don't go judging all Fundamentalists by a handful of Fundamentalist wackos with Web sites.

To keep doors open is to invite messiness, complication, and worse.

"You shut the door of the kingdom of heaven in people's faces."

Read Matthew 23—the whole chapter.

• **Bibles commonly subtitle** the section beginning in verse 13 as "The Seven Woes on the Teachers of the Law and the Pharisees," or something similar.

• **In a nutshell, what are the seven woes?** What seven things did Jesus condemn the teachers and the Pharisees for?

WOE 1:

WOE 2:

WOE 3:

WOE 4:

WOE 5:

WOE 6:

WOE 7:

• **Parts of the tongue-lashing** Jesus gave the Pharisees have worked their way into popular understanding and usage.

~ "You strain out a gnat but swallow a camel." (verse 24)
~ "You are like whitewashed tombs…." (verse 27)
~ "You brood of vipers!" (verse 33)

What did Jesus mean by each of these metaphors?

• As you've seen, **Jesus gets a little intense** in this episode. What does he say to the Pharisees in the following verses that isn't exactly in line with the Gentle Shepherd image of Jesus?

verse 15:

verse 27:

verse 33:

• **In fact, Jesus essentially condemns** these particular teachers and Pharisees to hell.

~"You yourselves do not enter [the kingdom of heaven], nor will you let those enter who are trying to." (verse 13)

~"How will you escape being condemned to hell?" (verse 33)

How do such statements influence your personal version of Jesus? What happened to the loving, grace-giving Lord?

Finally...

• Anything in these verses that's a puzzle to you? That just doesn't make sense?

• What one thing got your attention most of all in these verses? Why did it affect you like it did?

Talk about opening and closing doors

• Have you ever felt that you shut a door on someone else? Excluded that person in the name of God? How sincere did you feel you were at the time? In retrospect, can you imagine yourself having done any differently?

• Ever had a religious or spiritual door shut on you? If you want to, talk about that.

• What do you think of what Jesus says often in the Gospels: embezzlers and inside-traders (what the first-century tax collectors essentially were) and prostitutes were entering the kingdom of heaven—and influential, proud religious leaders (the Pharisees, the teachers of the law, the chief priests, etc.) weren't? What do you believe that says about *today's* financial scandal defendants and the streetwalkers in your city's red-light district? About *today's* influential religious leaders?

> The following passages may inform your discussion.
> ~ Matthew 21:31
> ~ Mark 2:15-17
> ~ Luke 7:36-50

• In the song "Kingdom" Lost And Found sings,

> So many people pushed away
> Ones that are loved told they can't stay....

Where does your church draw the line? Where do *you* draw the line? That is, what kind of person or people would make you feel like they don't belong there in church with you?

• Respond to the following comparisons between Jesus' culture and yours. Talk with each other about your responses, and why you responded the way you did.

THEN—a religious culture where lepers were contagious untouchables
WHAT JESUS DID—touched them, healed them (Matthew 8, Mark 1, Luke 5)
NOW—a religious culture where sufferers of HIV/AIDS are contagious untouchables
WHAT SHOULD YOU DO? (Make your mark wherever along the line best represents your belief or feelings.)

●──●

Nothing, because I don't agree with the premise that modern HIV/AIDS is anything like leprosy of ancient times.	The two diseases seem to occupy a similar place in both cultures...but aren't most HIV/AIDS cases the result of homosexual sin? Shouldn't that affect how we treat them?	Exactly what Jesus did. Victims of HIV/AIDS need whatever touch, love, care, and healing that Christians can bring to them.

THEN—a culture where the ethnic minority Samaritans were suspect, unwanted, and the object of prejudice and racism
WHAT JESUS DID—relaxed and chatted with them (John 4:1-42), and used them as an example of godly mercy (Luke 10:25-37)
NOW—a culture where—still, in many areas and to varying degrees—African Americans, American Islamics, legal and illegal alien Hispanics, etc., are suspect, unwanted in many areas, and the object of prejudice and racism
WHAT SHOULD YOU DO? (Make your mark wherever along the line best represents your belief or feelings.)

●——●

| Nothing, because I don't agree with the premise that modern Islamics, etc., are anything like what the Samaritans were in ancient Palestine. | What Jesus did is the ideal, and what we should strive for—but modern realities complicate things. The world is not as simple as it used to be, and Jesus understands that. | Exactly what Jesus did—overcome local racism (however subtle or overt), befriend those in other ethnic groups, and recognize the spiritual goodness they bring to a culture. |

THEN—a religious culture whose tax collectors and prostitutes were considered equally immoral, and so were equally ostracized by that religious culture
WHAT JESUS DID—went into the houses of these sinners to socialize with them, and then made friends and disciples of them (Matthew 9:10-13; Luke 7:36-50; Luke 15:1-2; Luke 19:1-7)
NOW—a religious culture in which gay individuals and skinheads are considered as immoral as prostitutes, and so are equally shunned by that religious culture
WHAT SHOULD YOU DO? (Make your mark wherever along the line best represents your belief or feelings.)

●——●

| Nothing, because I don't agree with the premise that today's gays or skinheads are the modern equivalent of 1st-century Judean tax collectors and prostitutes. | Even if I had any desire to socialize with gay people or skinheads—which I don't—I wouldn't know where to start. I think Jesus is satisfied when I befriend an unpopular classmate at school. | Exactly what Jesus did—learn to socialize and befriend those that one's religious culture shuns, including gays and skinheads. |

A Brief History of Ecclesiastical Door Shutting

In this resource cluster:
• A concise and entertaining Christian church history, from the beginning to the Jesus Movement...how exclusion leads to splintering which, in turn, leads to new churches...plus teaching points *(A Church-Splinter Primer)*
• A Bible study: Acts 15—the Council at Jerusalem *(Early Church Crisis)*
• Discussion-starting Qs *(Talk about church splintering and closed doors today)*

teaching points

A Church-Splinter Primer

Most of us spend too much time on the last twenty-four hours and too little on the last six thousand years.
[Will Durant, "September 11, 2001," *The Sun*, October 2001]

> To create a wise future in our churches, we need to know our past— even the unsavory parts.

Let us look at whence we came. Your spiritual roots, your faith journey is not just *yours*, but follows a compass bearing determined by generations of Christians before you. (And the events in *your* life and the decisions *you* make contribute to whatever direction the faith journeys take of people you influence.)

If for no other reason than to keep us humble and alert to the door-shutting tendencies in us, this primer is offered not to badmouth Christianity, but to illustrate 1) how our spiritual forebears were as inclined to shut doors on people as any virgin-sacrificing pagan or hardboiled atheist, and 2) how, even knowing all this, Christ is still comfortable using this cauldron of misguided motives and screwy methods and flawed people—i.e., his church—to do his work in this world.

Plus, perhaps being reminded of the darker side of our ecclesiastical history may help us keep from repeating it.

The cycle
What we see in the history of Christianity, as it blossomed in the Middle East, then spread into Europe and Africa, and later spread to the Americas, is a cycle as predictable as anything Marx and Engels could have devised. In a sentence: *When an oppressed minority becomes dominant, it inevitably finds a new minority to oppress.* When people who have had doors shut on them finally become doormen themselves, they always seem to forget what it was like, and end up shutting doors on others.

> The apparent rule, if history is any clue: When an oppressed minority becomes dominant, it in turn oppresses a new minority.

> Christians in the early church weren't just excluded—they were persecuted, often to the death.

The Acts of the Apostles records the beginning of a tough couple of centuries for an embryonic Christianity. As you can read for yourself virtually anywhere you flip in this New Testament book, Christians are persecuted by both the Jewish and the Roman establishments—basically because their beliefs undermine the control these two ancient bastions of authority hold over the populace. Even when Christians are seen to be quiet and law-abiding citizens, they become convenient scapegoats for a city's ills.

Yet Christianity spreads like wildfire, in influence as well as in number of converts, until along comes a fourth-century Roman emperor, the great Constantine, who decrees an official policy of toleration of Christianity (and other cults). Finally, Christians no longer need fear arrests at midnight or colosseum crucifixions at midday. Thus begins several centuries of official and scholarly head scratching about which Christian beliefs are the Approved Beliefs and which interpretations are the Correct Interpretations.

Much of what we take for granted today as orthodox Christian doctrine was actually hammered out in a series of councils that drew Christian leaders and thinkers from all corners of the Mediterranean world. The dark side of all that, however, is that, at the time, those individuals and churches who found themselves on the far side of council decisions either had to adjust their beliefs or be turned out of the church as heretics. Or, in the case of some, create their own church so they could continue in their beliefs.

Let the splintering begin.

East is east, and west is west...

The Christian church in the Mediterranean world split big when Rome (west) and Constantinople (east) became rival spiritual capitals. Rome became the fountainhead of Roman Catholicism, which spawned the various monastic orders (Dominican, Franciscan, Benedictine, Jesuit, etc.), whose monks eventually took the Roman Catholic version of Christianity to all corners of Europe (Gaul, Ireland, Scandinavia). It was Roman Catholicism that the Protestant Reformation split from. In short, the western Christian church became a significant—and perhaps the dominant—cultural influence in western Europe and the western hemisphere.

Meanwhile, Constantinople evolved as the spiritual headquarters of eastern Christianity, known today as Orthodox (with a capital O) Christianity. This mother faith nurtured several eastern varieties of Christianity: Russian Orthodoxy, Greek Orthodoxy, and Serbian Orthodoxy among them. As with Roman Catholicism, Eastern Orthodoxy the religion could hardly be separated from the politics of a given Orthodox nation. Still can't, in some countries.

If you spend any time talking with Orthodox friends (Orthodox congregations, by the way, have been springing up in America's suburbs for the past couple decades), you'll find out in a hurry that Orthodox Christians draw a straight line from the apostles to their church—and consider Roman Catholicism a splinter (okay, a big splinter...okay, a plank) that broke away from their own, true Christianity.

Martin Luther's protest

This loyal and devout German priest of the Roman Catholic church may well have got a splinter in his hand while nailing his 95 Theses to the church door at Wittenberg. All he had in mind was to challenge a colleague in the city to a debate about some common church practices that disturbed him, which he thought ought to be reformed.

The emperor Constantine declared Christianity legal—a favor, kind of. Before long, Christian mobs were burning the homes of pagans, and non-Christians were considered disloyal citizens.

Typical issue: how exactly was Jesus also God? Was he a normal man, but with God's spirit within him? Or did the body God used to become Jesus only look like a physical body, but really wasn't?

The Coptic Church, an Ethiopian Christian sect, is one of these.

Christianity splits big into Eastern Orthodoxy and Roman Catholicism

It is interesting to note that Islam has been perceived to be the quintessential spiritual adversary (and consequently, political and military adversary) of both western and eastern Christianity since the Middle Ages. This, despite teachings to the contrary in both the Bible and the Koran—which neither knight nor sultan apparently read. Or maybe they read only the "good parts," which promised divine destruction to one's enemies.

The Reformation: Luther's attempts to reform his own Roman Catholic church resulted in continent-wide wars, and the loss of millions of people, acres, and lira from the Catholic church into the hands of Protestant, anti-Catholic churches.

England withdraws from the Roman Catholic church, and forms its own national church: the Church of England.

There were many dissenting groups in England who disagreed with the theology of the Church of England:

• Puritans (sought to purify the Anglican church from within);

• Separatists (believed the Anglican church to be beyond help, and that the only righteous thing to do was to withdraw from it altogether).

English dissenters arrived in New England, where they hoped for religious freedom for themselves (but seldom gave it to others).

Roger Williams, lapsed Puritan—Rhode Island

Minority Catholics in American colonies—Maryland

William Penn, American visionary, built a city where toleration actually worked—Philadelphia, Pennsylvania

For a number of reasons, the reform that Luther desired—his protest against papal excesses and materialistic motives of some churchmen—exploded into a full-blown revolution that, to Luther's profound disappointment, civil leaders quickly exploited for their own political advantage. The Thirty Years War, ostensibly between continental Protestant and Catholic forces, led to the massacre of several millions of soldiers and civilians, and—as most wars said to be wars of religion—was not about faith, but civil sovereignty, power, and control of people, taxation, and political borders.

During this time England seesawed between Protestant and Catholic monarchs, each one in turn burning and beheading members of the opposition. England eventually settled on Protestantism (by creating its own state church, the Church of England, or Anglican Church—which when exported to the American colonies became the Episcopal Church). True to the human condition, just as renegade Protestants from William Tyndale to Hugh Latimer were persecuted by the state, so other Protestants who dissented from the Church of England were persecuted, their property confiscated, the males imprisoned—or worse. So did Protestant England not only to the Catholics losers, but also to dissidents within their own Protestant fold.

The Puritans were such a persecuted group—until they got politically savvy, started gaining seats in Parliament, and soon replaced the Church of England as the dominant political and religious influence.

The Puritans, however, remembered their difficult early days as a devout, God-fearing Christian sect, and so the Puritan government let all Englishmen and women worship as they wanted.

You didn't really believe that, did you? Good. The Puritans immediately began to persecute dissenters within *their* ranks, including the Separatists, who called themselves Pilgrims because they got tired of Puritan England imprisoning them and confiscating their homes, and fled first to Holland, and then to America, looking for a land in which they could worship freely.

One nation, under God (but it had better be *my* God)

On this side of the Atlantic, in New England, the later-arriving Puritans soon absorbed the small Separatist towns into their own and picked up in the New World where they left off in the Old. The Puritans were all for religious freedom—for themselves, that is. The fact that some had their own theological ideas, or biblical interpretations, only confirmed to the Puritan fathers that faithless heretics or witches lived among them. So they hanged the witches and exiled the heretics.

Roger Williams was one of those, and modern American Baptists consider him their spiritual forebear. He fled south and was instrumental in founding the colony that would be known as Rhode Island.

The few Catholics in America, meanwhile, were as spiritually and politically suspect here as they were in England. Still, they managed to create a haven for themselves in the colony of Maryland. They would also have found a welcome in Philadelphia, the City of Brotherly Love, founded and designed by William Penn, who aimed to create a civil government that tolerated Americans of any or no religion—and he really meant it. Quakers, Catholics, Baptists, Jews—the fringe element of the colonial religious establishment—lived, worked, and worshiped in peace in Philadelphia like no where else in America at that time.

With political independence from England also came religious independence. The Constitutional Convention included the separation-of-church-and-state clause in the First Amendment to ensure that church membership and religion (or lack of either or those) would not affect the rights of U.S. citizenship. Convention delegates were, of course, thinking of England, where baptized members of the Church of England were considered patriots, and non-members (especially Roman Catholics) were suspected of disloyal, treasonous sentiments.

With no governmental constraints on personal religion, characteristic American individualism quickly showed itself: within the next 150 years, Protestant denominations in this country multiplied, splintered, recombined, splintered again. (Case in point: there are more than two dozen official varieties of Baptists in the U.S., including Duck River [and Kindred] Association of Baptists, Seventh-Day Baptists, and Primitive Baptists. And no, the Cooperative Baptist Fellowship is no oxymoron.) Brand-new denominations and sects flourished in this fertile American religious soil: Mormon, Jehovah's Witness, various Pentecostal, Seventh-Day Adventist, and Christian Science are among the better-known divisions. The Roman Catholic church, meanwhile, never quite lost its foreign, un-American associations (an Italian pope dictated doctrine for American Catholics, after all), and it has remained a secondary religious force in the U.S. to this day.

The Jesus movement

This 1970s phenomenon redirected and redefined American religion as much as any of the earlier awakenings or national revivals. This movement achieved something of a miracle: it joined three hitherto very separate and often hostile forces: evangelical Bible teaching and exposition (the Protestant cerebral), Pentecostal fervency (the Protestant visceral), and rock music (the Protestant whipping boy—the epitome of worldliness). Within a couple decades, what had been demonized as "hippie influences"—long hair, guitars and drum sets, shorts and sandals—became acceptable in Sunday worship services in all kinds of churches across the country, mainline, independent, even Roman Catholic parishes. The simple choruses and songs of charismatic worship became the "praise music" eventually used even by staid Baptist and Lutheran congregations.

In short, a basic, practical division between most Protestant churches in America could be this: those that embrace at least some of the characteristics of the Jesus Movement (perhaps without knowing where their worship style derives from), and those that shun such practices and worship styles.

Despite a quarter century of increasing commonality, splintering is still in the air:

• Leadership of the Southern Baptists, America's largest denomination, regularly divides over the issue of biblical inerrancy.
• Although officially the United Methodist Church recognizes neither same-sex marriages nor the ordination of gay clergy, many UMC churches have bucked the parent denomination and become "reconciling churches" that advocate "for inclusion of people of all sexual orienta-

Bill of Rights: separation of church and state (i.e., no people should be made to feel uncomfortable or un-American because of their religion or lack of it)

American individualism is apparent even in religion: for two centuries churches divide and multiply, creating, in the process, what orthodox Christianity labels "sects" or "cults."

Fast-forward to 1970: political and social nonconformity of the Vietnam and Watergate eras eventually reaches even into religion...

...and in some ways, the Jesus movement actually opened doors as it combined aspects of Christianity instead of splintering, and dividing.

"Jesus people"—or those influenced by them— grow up and become church leaders.

Yet religious bodies are still inclined to shut doors and exclude.

tions and gender identities as full participants in the United Methodist Church both in policy and practice." Needless to say, many other UMC churches believe strongly otherwise and zealously toe the denominational line.

• Presbyterians for Renewal, on the other hand, believes that its denomination—Presbyterian Church (USA)—has tipped way too far to the left when it comes to theological and social issues like homosexuality and abortion, and it works to return the PCUSA to its traditionally more conservative path.

Some splintering is deliberate and actually positive.

Splintering in evangelical churches commonly takes the shape of the infamous "church splits"—the result of rancor over church polity, pastoral adultery, and plain old personality clashes. But lately one is hearing more about some very deliberate, strategic, and positive "splintering" in evangelical circles:

• Some large, metropolitan "parent" churches "birth" new, small congregations that meet in strip malls, schools, or homes. Such "church plants" are intended to expand or duplicate the successful ministry of the parent church.
• A handful of large evangelical churches in the country—so-called megachurches like Willow Creek of suburban Chicago and Saddleback of Southern California—have marketed their high-growth model of ministry with products and conferences and, consequently, have their own little solar systems of like-minded churches in orbit around them, usually unofficially but no less loyally.
• A more contractual relationship exists among so-called "franchise" churches like the Vineyard and Calvary Chapel churches. They'd say their associations of member churches are "fellowships," not denominations.

This is the body of Christ

However divisive and door-shutting the Christian church has been, Jesus still uses it as his primary means of making himself known in this world.

Like it or not, the Christian church—with all its fussing and feuding, with its splits and its recombinations—is the means in this world by which Jesus has determined to make himself known. Yet the Christian church is composed of humans, after all, and so has always been only a step away from using its high purpose to shut its doors in the face of the "sinners," the "disobedient," the "unbiblical," the "backsliders," etc.

It's a tendency we can avoid in our own churches only if we know how easy it is to slip into. Because at the time, it always feels so right and so righteous.

"We should not make it difficult for the Gentiles who are turning to God."

Read Acts 15—the entire chapter. *(Hey, it's only 41 verses...and people get ticked off at each other in the chapter, too. Good reading!)*

• **A little background:** Paul and Barnabas had just returned from their first trip abroad to preach the gospel. Early in that trip they changed their "target"; after you read Acts 13:44-48, you can understand why Paul and Barnabas were in "sharp dispute and debate" with what they heard when they got back home to Jerusalem (Acts 15:1-2).

• **Did you notice** who was at this council of Christians, among others? Read verse 5 again. What are they doing here? Weren't the Pharisees the bad guys? Apparently not so bad that they couldn't become Christians *and* remain Pharisees. Even as Christians, they're still firm believers in the law of Moses.

• **When Peter got up to speak** (verses 7-8), he was alluding to a life-changing experience of his, recorded in Acts 10. God had to be downright dramatic to convince Peter—and later the leaders of the Jerusalem church—that non-Jews as well as Jews could become Christians. So Peter immediately understood what Paul and Barnabas were talking about and sided with them in the debate.

• Summarize the **two sides of this debate** in your own words:

~ Christian Pharisees:

~ Paul, Barnabas, Peter:

• **Judging from council leader** James' decision (verses 19-21)—a decision repeated in his letter to believers in the surrounding area (verses 28-29)—who won the debate?

• What are **the four stipulations** that the council put on new non-Jewish believers?

• Do you think it was right for **James to declare a compromise** between the Pharisees' position, and Paul, Barnabas, and Peter's position? If it was right, why aren't today's non-Jewish converts to Christ—like you, most probably— required to keep those same four restrictions?

• Verses 30-35 reflect **a lot of satisfaction** with James' ruling. But what happens in verses 36-41 that returns us all to the reality of fallible humans trying to work with each other?

BONUS LOOK-UP
• Even earlier, the church had successfully averted some splintering. Read Acts 6:1-7. What was the issue? Who had the grievance? Why? What decision was made? Do you think it was a reasonable judgment?

Talk about church splintering and closed doors today

• Has a church, a religious organization, or a leader of one of those ever shut a door on you? If you want to, talk about that.

• Do you believe there's a door that your church *ought* to shut on someone? Or a kind of someone on whom the church ought to shut a door?

• What do you think keeps several small churches in your town or neighborhood from joining forces and cooperating in the gospel mission they all say they believe in? What would it take for them to stop duplicating efforts, consolidate their ministries, and make an impact on your town or neighborhood that would be felt by everyone? Or would this even be a good thing?

To explore the following questions, you may want a church leader present who is familiar with your church's origins and history.

• What do you know of the origins of your own church? In what year or decade did it begin? What were the circumstances of its birth? Was it a splinter from another church?

• If your church is part of a denomination or nationwide fellowship or association, what do you know of the origins of that denomination or fellowship?

• What is a current debate in your denomination? Which side do you agree with?

• What debate or dispute in your church was settled by a compromise? Did the compromise satisfy everyone? If not, what was the result?

The Visit

by Adrian Plass

Our church used to be very okay. We did all the things that churches do just about as well as they could be done, and we talked about our founder with reverence and proper gratitude. We said how much we would have liked to meet him when he was around and how much we looked forward to seeing him at some remote time in the future.

The unexpected news that he was going to pay us an extended visit now, in the present, was, to say the least, very disturbing. All confident statements about "the faith" tended to dry up. People who had always seemed reasonably cheerful looked rather worried. Those who had been troubled appeared to brighten considerably.

A man who had always said that "atonement is a peculiarly Jewish idea" became extremely thoughtful. Someone who had published a pamphlet entitled "The Real Meaning of the Resurrection Myth" joined the midweek prayer group and developed an open mind. Desperate folk just counted the days.

Each of us, I suppose, reacted to the news in our own way, but I think the thing we had in common was a feeling that the game (albeit a very sincere and meaningful game for some) was over. No more pretending when he came. He would know.

As for myself, I was looking forward to his coming, as long as it worked out "all right"—if you see what I mean. I was an organizer, a doer. My job was to keep the life of the church community tidy, make sure that the right people ended up in the right place doing the right things, and I enjoyed being good at it. Granted, I wasn't one of the super-spiritual types, but I smiled and sang with the rest on a Sunday and I seemed to be liked and respected by most folk. God? Well, I suppose my relationship with God was a bit like a marriage without sex—if I'm honest. I'd never got close. But—I worked hard, and I felt I must have earned a small bed-sit in heaven, if not a mansion.

So, my job was to organized our founder's visit, make sure it went smoothly, and generally mastermind the whole event. Before long I'd prepared a program for the day of his arrival and even sorted out whom he'd stay with. There was a little wrangling about who that should be. Somebody said that it should be a person who was the same at home as he was in church, and someone else said that in that case he'd have to stay in a hotel, but in the end I just chose who it would be and that was that.

My main problem was that I wasn't able to contact him in advance to talk about the arrangements. All I actually knew was that he would arrive for evening service on Sunday, but I wasn't worried. In my experience, visitors were only too pleased to slot into a clear order of events, and I assumed that he, of all people, wouldn't want to rock somebody else's carefully balanced boat. Isn't it odd when you look back and remember thinking ridiculous thoughts like that? At the time it seemed quite reasonable, and I was so used to tying up loose ends (even when there weren't any to tie sometimes), that it never occurred to me that somebody who embodied the very essence and spirit of creativity might, as it were, bring his own loose ends with him.

As the day of the visit drew closer, a sort of mild panic passed through the church. One person said that she felt a visit "in the flesh" lacked taste and was likely to corrupt the purity of her vision of God, another that in his view it was taking things "too far." One man, hitherto regarded as being a most saintly character, confessed to an array of quite startling sins, thus becoming, in the eyes of the church, less admirable but far more interesting and approachable. One sweet old lady cornered me on evening in the church room and anxiously asked me the question that probably troubled most of us: "Is it true that he knows...everything we think?"

I didn't know the answers to questions like that. I just wanted things to go well and looked forward, as I usually did, to the time when it was all over and we could look back and say, "It really went well," and, "Wasn't it worthwhile?" I'm afraid it was to be some time before I learned not to stash experiences safely away in the past before they had a chance to change me.

Anyway, Sunday arrived at last and sure enough—he came.

Now, I know it seems an awful thing to say, but at first it looked as if it was going to be a terrible disappointment—and anticlimax. He wasn't quite what we'd expected. He was rather too...real. His arrival was odd, too. I'd planned it to be quite an occasion, and maybe I was wrong, but I was hoping for something in the way of a grand entrance.

Everything was set up, everyone in their places, when we suddenly realized that the man we were waiting for was already there, sitting quietly in the back row. To be honest, I wouldn't have recognized him, but thank goodness, somebody did and suggested he come out to the front.

Well, I was just thinking, *Great, we can get started now,* but I hadn't even spoken to him when he turned to face the congregation and said (and you're not going to believe this), "Has anyone got a sandwich?" Well, a few people laughed, but one old lady went straight round the back to the kitchen and made him a sandwich and a cup of tea, and when she brought them back he sat down on the steps and enjoyed them without any sign of self-consciousness.

I was completely thrown by this. I'd got a copy of the program in my hand, but when I pulled myself together enough move toward him, he stood up, turned round and looked at me, and I just couldn't give it to him. I can't describe the look he gave me. It made me want to cry and hit him. That sounds ridiculous, doesn't it, but he made me feel like an idiot, and I admit that I felt oddly ashamed as well. But why?

Anyway, he turned to face all the people again and he looked at them as if he was looking for a friend in a crowd. He seemed to be searching for a face he knew. then someone waved to him and this is where the whole thing just got silly. He ran down the aisle and put his arms round this woman in the fourth row, and she was crying, and he was saying something to her that none of us could hear, and then some other people got up and went over to him until there was quite a little crowd with him in the middle of it.

It was weird. You see, there were people still sitting in their seats, still facing the front, obviously embarrassed and not knowing what to do, while over at the side was this knot of people laughing and crying and making one heck of a noise. Then...all the noise stopped. Quite suddenly, when he put his hand up, there was absolute silence.

Over at the other side of the church a young fellow was sitting, facing the front, and he seemed to be paralyzed. His face was white, his hands were clenched on his knees, and he seemed to be holding himself together by an effort of will. Then there were these two words that seemed to unlock him somehow.

"Don't worry." That was all. Just, "Don't worry," and that young fellow went flying across the church and skidded to a halt on his knees. And then it started all over again—the noise I mean—and then they all went out. They just...went out.

I followed them to the door, and I actually managed to catch hold of his coat sleeve. "Excuse me," I said, "I thought we were all going to be together for the service."

"Of course," he said and smiled, "please come with us."

I just didn't know what to do then. "But we usually have the service in church."

"Wouldn't you rather come with me?" he said.

Well, I would have really, but I didn't know where he was going to go. I thought he was going to fit in with us, and he seemed so...haphazard.

"Where *are* you going?" I asked.

He looked up and down the street (and here's another thing you won't believe), pointed across the street, and said, "What's that pub like?"

I said, "It's a bit rough really," and anyway, I knew for a fact that two or three of the people with him wouldn't go into a pub on principle. At least I thought I knew, because they all trailed in there after him; young fellows, maiden aunts, old men—the lot. I was stunned.

I stood by the church door for half an hour and round about half past seven he came out again, and I swear to you he had more people with him when he came out than when he went in. They all swarmed back over the road to the church and he said to me, "Can we come back in now?"

So they all came back in and sat down. Well, I say "sat down"—they hung themselves on the back of pews, sat cross-legged on the floor, draped themselves over the radiators, just anyhow, and he started to talk to them. (All the people who had stayed in the church had gone by then, including the lady he was supposed to be staying with.)

Now, this is the bit I don't understand. He'd spoiled my service, everything had gone wrong, and he'd made me feel really stupid, but more than anything I wanted to sit down on the floor and listen to him talk—and I got the feeling that he wanted me to.

But I didn't

I went home.

You know, I haven't cried, not really cried, since I was a little boy, but that night I sat at home and cried my eyes out. Then quite suddenly I knew what to do. I slammed out of the house and ran back to the church. It was so quiet when I got there, I though they must have all gone, but when I went in, there was just him sitting there. He smiled warmly.

"You took your time," he said, "I've been waiting for you. I'm staying at your house tonight."

From the short story "The Visit," in The Visit and Other Stories, *copyright 1991 by Adrian Plass (Zondervan). Reprinted by permission.*

ALL I'VE EVER WANTED

You are all I've ever wanted
You are all I've ever known
I've been lost all these
years 'til you came home

1. Ever since you went away
I've been waiting night and day
Oh I could have made you stay
But it would not be love that way
Sure you could go, but just so
you know...

2. You have always been free
And always a part of me
What was I supposed to do?

I would not put chains on you
Sure you could go, but just so
you know...

3. My beautiful one come
Winter's over and the rain is done
I see you now, my lovely one
Singing season has begun

You are all I've ever wanted
You are all I've ever known
I've been lost all these
years 'til you came home
I've been lost all these
years 'til you came home

There are no end of movies that illustrate constant, unwavering, solid-as-a-rock love or grace—especially when that love is unrecognized, ignored, or rejected. Cue up one or two or three of these clips before the meeting, and get your kids thinking down the groove of *constant, unfluctuating love*.

After showing the clip(s) draw kids' attention to that groove with questions like these (if students are familiar with the movie, as they probably are, their responses may be informed by other parts of the movie than just the clip you showed—which is great!):

- *In the clip you watched, who had the constant love?*
- *What did this constant lover overcome: rejection, distance, physical peril, skepticism, or what?*
- *What finally made the beloved give in and be loved?*

Here are the clip descriptions:

Toy Story (3 min. clip)

- **Reset counter** to 00:00:00 when the "20th Century Fox logo presents" appears on screen
- **Start clip: about 00:56:35**—Woody is trapped in blue milk crate
- **Stop clip: about 00:59:30**—Buzz says, "Let's get you outta this thing," and Woody replies, "Yes, sir!"
- **Key line:**

    Woody: "Over in that house is a kid who thinks you are the greatest, and it's not because you're a Space Ranger, it's because you're a *toy*."

The Princess Bride (4 min. clip)

- **Reset counter** to 00:00:00 when "Act III Communications Presents" appears on screen
- **Start clip: about 00:36:08**—Westley (masked in the black garb of the Dread Pirate Roberts) says, "Rest, Highness."
- **Stop clip: about 00:40:00**—Ill boy in bed says, "They're kissing again. Do we have to hear the kissing part?"
- **Key lines:**

    Westley: "Death cannot stop true love...what it can do is delay it a while."
    Buttercup: "I will never doubt again."
    Westley: "There will never be a need."

The Saint (4 min. clip)

• **Reset counter** to 00:00:00 when the Paramount logo appears on screen

• **Start clip: about 01:21:10**—Simon and Emma climb out of the underground water tunnel.

• **Stop clip: about 01:25:13**— Emma (safe within the gates of the U.S. embassy) and Simon catch each other's eyes through the flames of the explosion before he disappears into the night.

• **Key line:**

    Simon: "I'll find you...you found me."

God is Love–and a Lover

In this resource cluster:

• The romance of being loved by God...dark and light sides of sexual imagery in the Bible...plus teaching points (*Our Erotic Faith*)
• A Bible study: Song of Songs (*Arise, My Darling*)
• Discussion-starting Qs (*Talk about longing, love, God, and sex*)

teaching points

Our Erotic Faith (HUH?!)

Inability to love masks the terror of being touched. And if you can't be touched, you can't be changed. And if you can't be changed, you can't be alive.
[James Baldwin, from an interview by Jere Real, quoted in *Utne Reader*, Jul-Aug 2002, p. 100]

A good lover is a good kisser...a good lover is a reliable partner...a good lover is a good parent...a good lover is not defined by the loving relationship, though the relationship is defined by the lover...a good lover can receive without reciprocating....

And a good lover can give without receiving. Here (rather than in the good-kissing part) you have something that lies at the heart of humanity's most worthwhile endeavors: friendship, sacrifice, marriage, faith, child rearing, community. None of these works for long without grace of one sort or another. Only long-term, constant, and steady love can keep any of these relationships and institutions going for the long term.

One aspect of being a good lover is the ability to give without receiving in turn...

...which is what true love and grace are all about.

Lovers, destructive and otherwise

Of all the talk about love this and love that in the Bible, the romantic, sexual lover is one image of God you don't hear much about. In fact, romance and worship have a lot in common: the head-over-heels, all-consuming infatuation of both early romance and early conversion...the ecstasy in both lovemaking and the charismatic experience of many Christians...your attraction to someone besides your lover, be it attraction to another human or the lure of worldliness.

Not a lot of sermons on this: Bible writers' use of sexual metaphors to describe our relationship with God

Writers of the Bible are particularly explicit about this last metaphor, the spiritual femme fatale. In the opening chapters of Proverbs, the writer warns readers often against succumbing to the allure of adultery: "She took hold of him and kissed him...she said: '....I have perfumed my bed with myrrh, aloes and cinnamon. Come, let us drink deep of love till morning; let's enjoy ourselves with love! My husband is not at home; he has gone on a long journey.'" Many scholars believe that such sexual passages in Proverbs are primarily metaphorical, warning us away from one-night stands with the whore Folly and toward a lifetime with Lady Wisdom (who is consistently personified as a female—see Proverbs 4:6).

Dark mistresses of the Bible—and what they represent:

• adulterous wife (Proverbs 5; 6:20-35; 7);

Elsewhere in the Old Testament, when Israel falls away from Jehovah and trusts instead in alliances with neighboring powers, the nation is often described as a wandering wife who sleeps with other men. Chapters 16 and 23 of Ezekiel are downright graphic in their sexual imagery. And in John's vision of Revelation, Babylon the "mystery" is "the mother of prostitutes" with whom "the kings of the earth committed adultery" (Revelation 17)—to most interpreters, an obvious metaphor for a city or a power.

So much for the dark mistress, the lover who destroys you.

On the bright side of sexual imagery is the openly erotic Song of Songs, which in lush, sensual language describes the longings for and pleasures of unabashed sexual romance. There are enough breasts and thighs and mouths and arousal in this Bible book to keep a romance humming for a long time.

When you read Song of Songs, you can tell that the lovers are into each other for more than just a roll in the hay and a cigarette before going back to their families and the real world. You get the feeling that these lovers give their bodies to each other because they've given parts of their very selves to each other. Sex seals the commitment, reminds them of each other's constancy. Affection may fail now and then during their lives together (and you can believe there will be little sex at such times), but not their grace. Not their love.

In the New Testament, St. Paul unwraps another layer of meaning to all this sexual passion: the church is kind of like the bride, the lover of Christ, he writes. And husbands should love their wives with the same constancy, with the same unwavering grace with which Christ loves the church (Ephesians 5:25-33).

Seasons of love

It's a good thing God doesn't expect us to reciprocate his own passionate love and constant grace in kind. Your felt love for God ebbs and flows because of all sorts of things: how you feel about yourself, what you read, what you've eaten, how many tests you have this week, what time of day or season of the year it is.

And in many Christians, the timetable is all backwards, contrary to the popularized order of love events with God, which goes something like this:

- You ignore God, or actively dislike him.
- You get saved—and your love affair with the Savior begins.
- The early season of salvation is colored by newness, fervor, enthusiasm—in short, the romance of young faith. Spiritual passion spikes early.
- Then comes settling in. The spike of passion that characterized your romantic season levels out into a gradually maturing relationship with God.

Yet the experience of a lot of Christians contradicts this neat, logical

Sidenotes:
- Israel, the slutty wife of Jehovah (Ezekiel 16, 23);
- The whore Babylon, the mother of prostitutes (Revelation 17).

Then there's the bright side: the romantic sensuality of the Song of Songs.

In the New Testament, Christ is described as the lover of his bride, the church—that's us!

God's grace and love may be constant, but our love in return can be pretty fickle.

The popular timetable for the romance called salvation...

order. Some, for example, experience this:

...what an actual romance with God often looks like.

• You can hardly remember *not* being a Christian. It was in the air from your earliest memories, and you can't exactly say when it went from there into your heart.

• Christianity becomes an unconscious framework for how you perceive life. No passion here, just a matter-of-factness with which you interpret your world.

• In adolescence or young adulthood you awaken intellectually to your faith. Bible study, biblical languages, and the idealism of Christian community capture your imagination. A big spike here of love of learning about God, if not of spiritual passion.

• A decade or two or three later, your world comes undone, your tightly constructed theories about God unwind and get all tangled up, your battered theologies are reduced to "Jesus loves me, this I know"—and, for some reason, that is enough, and you find yourself crying often, at the drop of a hat—why, you're not sure—gratitude is part of it, and loss and yearning, and some of it feels like praying.

Welcome to your season of passion.

There is not one correct or preferred path to Christian passion. The romance of faith hits some early, others late. And it's all good, because God our lover knows our tolerances, knows when we're ready and when we're not, and in the meantime fills us with little premonitions of what's waiting for us. It all adds up to this life, which is, of course, one big Premonition of the life to come: a never-ending life of love in the presence of the constant Lover.

There's no one correct path to Christian passion. It takes you, you don't take it.

"The winter is past; the rains are over and gone."

Read Song of Songs 2:10-13. *Read ONLY this passage. DO NOT READ ANY OTHER PART OF THIS BOOK. RATED R. CONTAINS EROTIC REFERENCES TO MOUTHS, THIGHS, AND BREASTS. IN FACT, WE'RE NOT ALL THAT CONVINCED THAT THIS BOOK ACTUALLY BELONGS IN THE BIBLE.*

• **Oh, all right.** You can read the good parts of this love poem, too, but no giggling. This book is a wedding song of sorts, that celebrates erotic love between a new husband and wife. So if you can't deal with two people enchanted with the body parts of their beloved, don't read the book. (Don't worry—there's nothing explicit below the waist in this book. *Implied*, but not explicit.)

> [10] My lover spoke and said to me,
> "Arise, my darling,
> my beautiful one, and come with me.
> [11] See! The winter is past;
> the rains are over and gone.
> [12] Flowers appear on the earth;
> the season of singing has come,
> the cooing of doves
> is heard in our land.
> [13] The fig tree forms its early fruit;
> The blossoming vines spread their fragrance.
> Arise, come, my darling;
> my beautiful one, come with me."

• **Fig trees and vines** may not be your idea of a romantic setting, but, to ancient Israelis, they were as romantically evocative as roses and orchids are to us today. (Every culture has its own idea of what's erotic, suggestive, romantic. What's a turn-on in our culture is gross and repulsive to some other cultures. In some Polynesian cultures, obesity was beautiful, even erotic—and the queen needed to be the most beautiful of all. So as you read Song of Songs, remember that it reflects a culture far removed from yours, in both place and time, but no so far in other ways.)

• **Still, what are some romantic aspects** of this passage that reflect what is considered romantic in our culture?

• **Recognize any lyrics** from the Lost And Found song "All I've Wanted" in these Bible verses? Are the words appropriate to the song? Why or why not?

• It is said that **the theologian Pierre Benoit**, while praying over the Gospel of Luke for many years, believed God spoke the words in these verses to Jesus while hanging on the cross. What in this Song of Songs passage makes that interpretation possible?
    Read the last words of Jesus in Luke 23. If you were making a movie that reflected Benoit's belief, where in that chapter would you insert these Song of Songs words?

Finally...

• Anything in these verses that's a puzzle to you? That just doesn't make sense?

• What one thing got your attention most of all in these verses? Why did it affect you like it did?

Talk about longing, love, God, and sex

• In your small group, take turns tracing your own spiritual romances with God. When did you first sense him loving you? If you have felt passionate about God, when did that begin?

• Would you characterize your relationship with God as a love affair? Why or why not?

• The Lost And Found song says, "You're all I've ever wanted." Have you ever felt that way? Talk about that. Or do you feel like a second-class Christian because you *don't* feel that strongly?

• Were you surprised by the sexual and erotic references that you discovered in the Bible during this lesson? Why do you think our society tends to make God and sexuality opposites, even enemies?

Poetry option

Ask a good poetry reader to read aloud this sonnet by the 17th-century Christian poet John Donne:

> Batter my heart, three-personed God; for you
> As yet but knock, breathe, shine, and seek to mend;
> That I may rise and stand, o'erthrow me, and bend
> Your force to break, blow, burn, and make me new.
> I, like an usurped town, to another due,
> Labor to admit you, but O, to no end;
> Reason, your viceroy in me, me should defend,
> But is captived, and proves weak or untrue.
>
> Yet dearly I love you, and would be loved fain,
> But am betrothed unto you enemy.
> Divorce me, untie, or break that knot again;
> Take me to you, imprison me, for I,
> Except you enthrall me, never shall be free,
> Nor ever chaste, except you ravish me.

• This sonnet has two parts, each with its own imagery:
  ~ In the first 8 lines, the poet compares himself to a besieged city.
  ~ In the last 6 lines, the poet compares himself to a woman who wants to be taken.

• The speaker wants to be taken by whom? From whom? And what is the sexual irony of the last two lines?

• How accurate do you feel this is? To what degree does it reflect real life? Real faith?

NEW CREATION

I wanna be a new creation
Formed from the fingers of God's right hand (yeah)
I wanna be a new creation
God's gonna make me stand

1. I want to see like Daniel
I want to love like John
I want to hope like Mary
I want to be the rock that's built upon
I want to laugh like Sarah
I want to preach like Paul
I want to live like Lazarus
Play my trumpet and watch the crumbling wall

2. I want to trust like Noah
I want to see like the man born blind
I want to pray like Simeon prayed
I want to be the coin that the finder finds
But if I never move the mountain
And if I never part the sea
And if I never slay the giant
God do what you want with me
God do what you want with me

Transform This

Before this session photocopy enough copies of the **Transform *This*** handout (page 89) for your group (one per student).

Here are the answers:

1. Blue
2. Gold
3. Pink or Wine
4. Gray
5. Ruby
6. Amber or umber
7. Brown
8. Coral
9. Green
10. Ocher
11. Olive
12. Rouge
13. Bronze
14. Cherry
15. Orange
16. Rose
17. Yellow
18. Scarlet

The Transform Norm

In this resource cluster:
• 3 kinds of transformation...how transformation works, what it looks like...plus teaching points
(*How You're New, How You're Not*)
• A Bible study of people who were transformed, changed profoundly in some way, a part of them made new: Sarah, Daniel, Mary the mother of Jesus, Simeon, the man born blind and healed by Jesus (*It's a New Life from Here On*)
• Discussion-starting Qs (*Talk about being changed, being transformed, being made new*)

teaching points	How You're New, How You're Not
	trans-form (v.t.)
Three definitions of the verb "transform"	1. *To change the form of; to change in shape or appearance; to metamorphose; as, a caterpillar is ultimately* transformed *into a butterfly.* 2. *To change into another substance; to transmute; as, the alchemists sought to* transform *lead into gold.* 3. *To change in nature, disposition, heart, character, or the like; to convert.*
Which definition most closely describes the transformation that begins with one's Christian conversion?	When one becomes a Christian via that phenomenon we call *conversion* (see chapter 2, "The Paradox of Conversion," page 31), a transformation begins. Good Christians disagree about what that transformation looks like (it is likely that bad ones do, too). You might as well throw a cat into a dog kennel as ask a roomful of theologians which of the three Webster definitions above best describes the transformation of a Christian.

3 kinds of transformations

• Transformed appearance...

...tends to be on the arbitrary side.

Take definition one, for instance. A lot of Christians maintain that our faith ought to show itself in our appearance. If unbelievers are pierced and tattooed, then piercings and tattoos become a worldly style that Christians should not identify with. If a "rebellious" subgroup in society sports heavy mascara or dyed hair, Christians (it is believed) are obliged to avoid those fashions. The motto of these Christians: If you're gonna call yourself a Christian, then for Pete's sake *look* like a Christian.

• Transformed substance...

...tends to be on the idealistic side.

Definition two—an alchemical change into another substance altogether—is appealing. It would be very convenient, and not nearly as messy as real life, if a Christian were indeed changed substantially from one thing to another thing. The doctrine of transubstantiation, held by the Roman Catholic church, is kind of like this: the change of communion bread and wine into Christ's actual flesh and blood. Mystically, but literally. By similar thinking, some Christians believe that they become something completely, absolutely different from what they were as non-Christians. Which, if you believe it, can give you a perilous sense of invulnerability, or at least set you up for a lot of disappointment.

• Transformed heart...

Definition three is the least measurable but the most influential of the three kinds of transformation: it is a change not of substance, but of disposition, heart, or character. This kind of change goes deep, and it may not be seen readily in a casual glance. This kind of change tends to seep out of you rather than pour out. This definition of transformation implies that appearances are neither here nor there, and that the actual substance that is you probably doesn't change—but the energy inside that substance, the motivations and imaginations that propel you through life are new, different, changed. Transformed.

This last definition rings true for a lot of Christians, especially when they take a long, realistic look at themselves. You are probably a very different person from what you were 10 or 20 or 30 years ago—but at the same time you have not changed at all. Just look at your deepest habits, your inclinations...the kind of people you enjoy being around...a season of the year that you love or loathe...whether you usually prefer company or solitude. Some things about a person never change. Some things are always changing.

What does transformation look like?

So what sorts of things can you expect to change when you become a Christian, and what sorts of things should you probably *not* expect to change?

The fruit of the Spirit is a starting point. Love, joy, peace, patience, kindness, goodness, faithfulness, gentleness, self-control—these qualities start deep in one's heart, in one's character. You cannot fake these, at least not for long. They start in the core of your being, and move outward through consciousness and muscle and skin until joy and goodness and self-control hit air and influence others.

And like most aspects of spirituality, transformation is a mix of *being acted upon* and *acting yourself.* You as a Christian cannot generate the kind of love, joy, peace, etc., that delights God and others without first having had the seed of Christ planted in you, that makes that fruit possible. On the other hand, God will not force his fruit to grow in you. You've got to consciously cultivate that seed into fruit that breaks into the light of day and actually does some good for and in others.

You can see this Both-And quirk of transformation in the individuals mentioned in the Lost And Found song "New Creation." Daniel had a visionary gift, that's for sure. But it was *how* he used that gift that set him apart as much as the gift itself did. Time after time you can read in the book of Daniel how kings offered him a CEO's salary and a seat among the royal advisors just for answers to a bizarre dream or event. Yet each time Daniel shrugged off the perks and concentrated on delivering accurate interpretations to the king. You can't keep a good man down, of course, and, at the end of his life, Daniel could say that he had worked in the top echelons of several Babylonian governments—but he earned those positions by his sterling reputation and native brilliance, not by accepting lavish gifts impulsively offered by a king desperate for answers.

Both-And. Inhaling-Exhaling. God gave Daniel the gift, and Daniel used it with tact, liberality, and humility. God gives you new life, and you are transformed as you exercise it.

...tends to ring true, seems to match what the Bible says and what your own experience tells you.

If transformation is such an inner thing, how can you recognize it?

The fruit of the Spirit, for starters (Galatians 5:22-23)

Real transformation is planted by God, and cultivated by you.

Example: Daniel—Read or skim the first six chapters for repeated evidence of this prophet's diplomatic and humble use of the transforming gift of vision God had given him.

Use what God has given you—otherwise your transformation will be incomplete.

It's a New Life from Here On

"Therefore if anyone is in Christ, he is a new creation; the old has gone, the new has come!"

The Bible people listed below were transformed—profoundly changed for the rest of their lives—in one way or another. Choose two or three of the people, read the biblical accounts about them, and talk about stuff like this:

• *Can you put your finger on exactly what it was that transformed them?*

• *How did they show their transformation, that change somewhere in them?*

Or simply talk about people or events or phrases in these passages that catch your attention, that you particularly disagree with, that seem to answer something for you. You may want to jot down some insights you or your group comes up with, or something memorable that one of you may say.

• **Sarah**—Genesis 18:1-15; Genesis 21:1-7

• **Daniel**—Daniel 2 (the whole chapter...it's a long one, but a good one)

• **Mary the mother of Jesus**—Luke 1:26-56

• **Simeon**—Luke 2:21-38

• **A man born blind and healed by Jesus**—John 9 (the whole chapter...a quick read, with some sarcasm in it, even)

Finally...

• Anything in any of these verses that's a puzzle to you? That just doesn't make sense?

• What one thing got your attention most of all in these verses? Why did it affect you like it did?

Talk about being changed, being transformed, being made new

• If you are a Christian, was your conversion a slam-bang transformation, or a quiet and gradual thing for you? How do you feel about that?

•Think about the spiritual transformations you've experienced. Which one was the most profound to you? (It may or may not have been your conversion.)

• Choose one of your transformations. How did it change you? How are you different? Do you feel that the difference is a "newness"?

• Do you feel that a passerby, a classmate in the school hallway, a customer who sees you at work, someone on the bus—do you think that people like this should be able to tell you're a Christian by your appearance? Talk about this.

Transform This

Change one letter in each word to name a color.

Ex. WED   <u>RED</u>

1. BLUR   _____

2. GOOD   _____

3. PINE   _____

4. TRAY   _____

5. RUBS   _____

6. EMBER   _____

7. BLOWN   _____

8. MORAL   _____

9. GREED   _____

10. OTHER   _____

11. ALIVE   _____

12. ROUGH   _____

13. BRONTE   _____

14. SHERRY   _____

15. GRANGE   _____

16. ROME   _____

17. BELLOW   _____

18. STARLET   _____

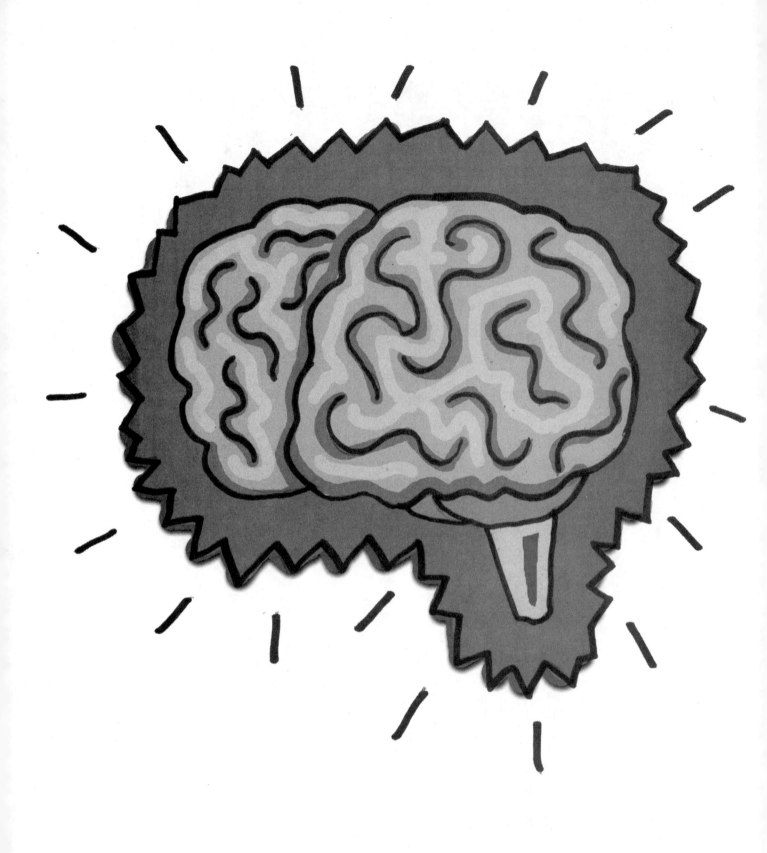

REMEMBER

Do not be afraid.
For the Love of God is displayed.
In this place, at this hour,
By God's grace and God's power.

1. Remember Eden's creation.
Remember the sign in the sky.
Remember the Father of Nations.
Gift of God upon Sinai.

2. Remember bread from heaven.
Remember water from stone.
Remember spring and new leaven,
and the promise of a permanent home.

3. Remember the answer to evil.
Everlasting love outpoured.
God is our God, and we are God's people.
God will remember our sin no more.

Meeting of Minds

If you remember the obscure '70s-era TV show hosted by Steve Allen called "Meeting of Minds," you'll recognize the general format of this script on page 101: four personages walk out of their own places in history and into our time, where they gather with a moderator and converse together in front of an audience.

What this conversation generally explores is the presence of God even in uncertain or just plain wretched circumstances—and how *remembering* your earlier encounters with God is a means for God's grace to comfort or empower you.

You can turn this script to any one of a number of purposes, and modify its content or its delivery in any way you want:

• Have students or adult volunteers deliver the script.

• Rehearse it for a polished performance, or have good and expressive readers read it cold.

• If you want to make a big splash for a big event, memorize the script. Or just do it readers theater style.

• Whether memorized or read, the script is suitable for everything from a retreat or camp (i.e., more of a performance) to a simple reading among the half-dozen members of your small-group Bible study in your living room.

• The moderator in this script is Barbara Walters, but you can use anyone you want: Ted Koppel, Conan O'Brien, a youth group student, yourself, etc.

Remembering Is Half the Battle

In this resource cluster:
• Why remembering is so central to faith, and biblical examples of this...plus teaching points (*Remembering*)
• A Bible study on Old Testament memorials (*Rock Memories*)
• Discussion-starting Qs *(Talk about why we remember, what we remember, how we remember)*

teaching points

The act of remembering connects us with our past (family past, spiritual past, any past) as well as gives us hope for our present and future.

Much of Judaism and Christianity is simply remembering—especially remembering how God's grace rescued us from this or that.

Examples:

• rainbow

• Jewish Passover

• Christian communion

Remembering

A dog's short-term memory, we are told, is about two minutes. Which means if you want to correct a dog's behavior, you've got two minutes to connect your correcting efforts with your pet's doggy sins. After two minutes, Rex won't have the faintest idea in his small, furry brain what it is you're talking about.

Humans do better at this than dogs, but even we need help remembering. When you imagine fire or flood forcing you to flee your house, why is it that heirlooms and family photos are among the first things you imagine scooping up on your way out the front door? Probably because they're reminders of our past, because such objects and images keep us connected with where we've come from.

Which may be why God, too, makes such a big deal about our remembering—especially remembering past acts of God's grace to us. When God's grace seems farthest away, when the night is blackest and hope is nowhere to be seen, God says, *Remember.*

Biblical commemorations
Take the rainbow, for instance. It's one big, gaudy sky-message that announces to all who see it, *REMEMBER!* Remember that although the world was once destroyed by water, it will not be again. (Your eschatology may tell you that the world will indeed be destroyed again—but not, if you take Genesis 9:14-15 literally, by water.)

Or Passover, Judaism's annual celebration of that pivotal event that marks year one on the Jewish calendar. Just about everything about Passover is intended to remind Jews of their deliverance and salvation from slavery in Egypt. The modern Seder meal, for example, is loaded with symbolism: the flat, yeastless bread is a reminder of the haste with which the Jews ate and ran; the haroset (an apple-cinnamon condiment) represents the mortar the Jewish slaves were forced to make for Egyptian construction projects.

It was the Passover Seder, of course, that Jesus ate with his 12 closest disciples in the upper room—and which Jesus invested with an additional layer of significance for Christians. "This is my body given for you; do this in remembrance of me," he said as he broke the *afikomen* matzah. "This cup is the new covenant in my blood, which is poured out for you," Jesus said as he passed the Cup of Redemption around the table. An aid to remember not only deliverance from Egypt, but now deliverance from sin and death.

The book of Esther narrates the reason for the Jewish festival of Purim. Esther, you may remember, was instrumental in saving expatriate Jews in

• Esther and Purim (read about the establishment of the holiday in Esther 9:20-28)

• ancient Jewish memorials (often a pile of rocks)

Joshua 4:1-8

• the Psalms

• Sunday

• your own B.C. days (before Christ)

Bottom line: do whatever it takes to remember Jesus, raised from the dead.

Persia from annihilation. By the time Esther's story was recorded, the two days "of feasting and joy" was apparently being celebrated annually. The entire point of Purim was to never forget this episode of salvation from Israel's enemies.

Often in Israel's early days a prophet or a general would command that a stone altar be built, or that stones simply be stacked, in order to commemorate a battle won, a crisis averted, an enemy defeated. That pile of rocks was intended to stand for a long time if not forever, simply to remind passers-by of how God saved Israel right there at that very place. Case in point: first thing after Joshua got Israel across the Jordan River safe and dry, even during flood stage (thanks to a Red Sea-like miracle), he made sure that stones from the river bed were set up on the bank. Joshua explained why: "In the future, when your children ask you, 'What do these stone mean?' tell them that the flow of the Jordan was cut off before the ark of the covenant of the Lord," the general said, adding, "These stones are to be a memorial to the Lord forever."

The Psalms—that national songbook of Israel—is essentially a poetic summary of all the things God has done for his people. Consider especially the "historical Psalms" (77, 78, 105, and 106): for centuries after the actual events, Jews and Christians have chanted and sung what Miriam first sang on the far shore of the Red Sea...have remembered how God delivered Jacob and Joseph...how God "led [his] people like a flock by the hand of Moses and Aaron"...how God fed and watered Israel in the desert...how he put up with Israel's faithlessness yet never abandoned them. As King David remembered God's past acts for the benefit of his nation, the singer-songwriter felt more hope for his own present and future.

Even Sunday, the traditional Christian day of worship instead of the original, seventh-day Sabbath—i.e., Saturday—is a reminder of what the first day of the week represents: Easter! The first day of the week—all 52 weeks' worth of them—is intended to be a little Easter, a weekly reminder of the resurrection of Jesus.

St. Paul even wanted the Ephesian Christians actually to remember their bad ol' days: "Remember that at that time you were separate from Christ," the apostle wrote, "excluded from citizenship in Israel and foreigners to the covenants of the promise, without hope and without God in the world." If Christians forget that, how can they appreciate having "been brought near through the blood of Christ"? (2:12-13).

Maybe it all comes down to what St. Paul wrote to his protégé Timothy: "Remember Jesus Christ, raised from the dead, descended from David. This is my gospel..." (2 Timothy 2:8). Whatever rituals or habits or holidays or feasts or parties it takes to remember *that*, are worth doing. Regularly. Frequently. Lest we forget.

Rock Memories

"These stones are to be a memorial to the Lord forever."

Read the three Bible passages listed below. Then talk about anything in the verses that catches your attention, that you particularly disagree with, that seems to answer something for you, that only complicates things for you, whatever. If you want some help, you may want to use the notes and questions following the Bible reference. And you might want to jot down some insights your group comes up with, or something memorable that one of you may say.

A dream—Genesis 28:16-22

A crossing—Joshua 4:1-8

A victory—1 Samuel 7:11-12

16When Jacob awoke from his sleep, he thought, "Surely the Lord is in this place, and I was not aware of it." 17He was afraid and said, "How awesome is this place! This is none other than the house of God; this is the gate of heaven."
18Early the next morning Jacob took the stone he had placed under his head and set it up as a pillar and poured oil on top of it. 19He called that place Bethel, though the city used to be a place called Luz.
20Then Jacob made a vow, saying, "If God will be with me on this journey I am taking, and will give me food to eat and clothes to wear 21so that I return safely to my father's house, then the Lord will be my God 22and this stone that I have set up as a pillar will be God's house, and of all that you give me I will give you a tenth."

—Genesis 28:16-22

1When the whole nation had finished crossing the Jordan, the Lord said, 2"Choose twelve men from among the people, one from each tribe, 3and tell them to take up twelve stones from the middle of the Jordan from right where the priests stood and to carry them over with you and put them down at the place where you stay tonight."
4So Joshua called together the twelve men he had appointed from the Israelite, one from each tribe, 5and said to them, "Go over before the ark of the Lord your God into the middle of Jordan. Each of you is to take up a stone on his shoulder, according to the number of the tribes of the Israelites, 6to serve as a sign among you. In the future, when your children ask you, 'What do these stones mean?' 7tell them that the flow of the Jordan was cut off before the ark of the covenant of the Lord. When it crossed the Jordan, the waters of the Jordan were cut off. These stones are to be a memorial to the people of Israel forever."
8So the Israelites sis as Joshua commanded them. They took twelve stones from the middle of the Jordan, according to the number of tribes of the Israelites; as the Lord had told Joshua; and they carried them over with them to their camp, where they put them down.

—Joshua 4:1-8

11The men of Israel rushed out of Mizpah and pursued the Philistines, slaughtering them along the way to a point below Beth Car.
12Then Samuel took a stone and set it up between Mizpah and Shen. He named it Ebenezer, saying, "Thus far has the Lord helped us."

—1 Samuel 7:11-12

• **Why this obsession** with stones when it came to marking important places in Old Testament times? How practical was it? How do modern societies commemorate events or places?

• In two of these three events, **a stone or a place** was given a name. What were those two names? What do they mean? What made the names appropriate to the situation?

• Which of the three men in question—**Jacob, Joshua, or Samuel**—actually proposed a deal with God instead of simply commemorating something God did for him? Talk about this.

• **Where did the stones in Joshua's story** come from? Why from there? Why 12?

DISCUSSION STARTERS

Talk about remembering

• What is remembered "officially" and regularly in your immediate or extended family? What rite if any is used as a memory aid?

• How does your church, or a church you've heard about, remember its milestone events?

• What fear of yours has been cooled by remembering something? What was it exactly you remembered?

• Recall right now some unmistakable instances of God's grace to you in the past. How can remembering these help calm present or future fears of yours?

The Difference Between Having Grace and Feeling Grace

In this resource cluster:
• How can God's grace be constant during those times you feel absolutely none of it?...plus teaching points *(Constant Grace, Even When You Don't Feel It)*
• A Bible study about when God is silent: Matthew 27 *(Did God Abandon His Son?)*
• Discussion-starting Qs *(Talk about the silence of the Lamb)*

teaching points

Like everything else in human experience, your feelings of closeness to God will also fluctuate.

Sin can cause this, of course...

...but so can simple (or complicated) physical and emotional conditions.

We always start energetically, and then tend to lose steam.

Constant Grace, Even When You Don't Feel It

Just because God's grace is constant—and in its constancy, a cure for fear—doesn't mean that you always feel or sense that grace. It's no secret that your experience of God's grace, of God himself, is up and down. Sometimes you're hot, sometimes you're not. Hot to hear God, that is, or hot to obey God, or talk about God, or talk *to* him, or learn more about him.

Sin can get in the way, of course. There's nothing like willingly and deliberately indulging in selfishness or anger or lust or gluttony or self-righteousness to make you feel a thousand miles from God.

But sin isn't the only thing that can make you feel distant from God, or lethargic about your spiritual life. Sometimes it's as simple as weariness (physical, emotional, any kind) or sleeplessness or extended ill health or a sudden change of diet or a move to a new, very different place. Or it may be something chemical or physiological.

But one reason for losing a sense of closeness with God, that just about all Christians experience sooner or later, is the ups and downs of being human. Being human means fluctuating in your feelings about your job, your marriage, your convictions, your diet. And your feelings of closeness to God.

The trick is, when you're in an inevitable season of spiritual disinterest, or in the middle of feeling like God has withdrawn from you—the trick is to not chuck it all, flush the whole Christian thing down the toilet, and spend your church offering on lottery tickets. It's not God, it's not even really *your* fault — it's just the fact of being human. Theologians call it "the human condition."

It's not just a spiritual thing. Usually at the start of something new—a friendship, a romance, a new job, a new group or team or association—your interest and energy are high, the newness can seem magical to you, you can't read enough about your new interest or club, or talk enough with your new friend. But whether within days or months or years, the newness fades, the job or club or friendship or romance loses its luster, and you gradually find that what at first came naturally and joyfully, now comes only with great effort—and often with no joy at all. Of course, at times like this you wonder why you're putting yourself through it all, and so you either leave the grind and start new at something else, or you resign yourself to staying with what's become a grind because of the trade-off: the thrill in your job or club may be gone, but you need the income, or you've already paid a year of dues and don't want to throw away the money, or something that keeps you mucking unenthusiastically through it.

Yet just as the law of the human condition states that this emotionally flat season is inevitable, it also states that it is not forever. In fact, your interest will fluctuate to a greater or lesser degree, and with longer or shorter periods, as long as you live.

All of which is to say, while God's grace is constant, your experience of it will not be. And there are some ironies about this for a Christian:

1. It is usually when you're in a flat season that you do the most amazing things for God.

2. It is usually in your flat seasons that you will grow the most spiritually.

3. It is your flat seasons, not your glory days, that make you an authentic person, a compassionate friend, a wise counselor, a mature Christian.

In classic Christian literature this flat season is known as "the dark night of the soul," a phrase coined by the 16th-century mystic St. John of the Cross. In modern Christian literature C.S. Lewis calls this the Law of Undulation, with its crests and troughs, described at the end of letter eight in *The Screwtape Letters*.

When you find yourself in such a flat season—a trough, a dark night of the soul—and it's reasonably clear to you and to those who know you well that God's silence to you is not due to anything you've done—when you find yourself there, there is really nothing to do but keep on keeping on. To hang in there. To believe against all believing that the grace of God that warmed you in earlier seasons of faith is still coming your way, but that, for whatever reason, you simply cannot sense it. Yet God will not seem silent forever. You will again feel his presence and his grace (which have been there all along, notwithstanding your sense of abandonment). You won't necessarily feel them in the same way, but you *will* feel them again.

And in the meantime, Jesus is walking with you through it all, albeit more quietly than you'd prefer.

"the human condition"

Being human means fluctuating…

…and this fluctuation affects how we sense God, even though God hasn't changed at all in his love for us.

In some ironic ways, we're the best Christians when we feel least like serving Christ but do it anyway.

"dark night of the soul"
(St. John of the Cross)

"the Law of Undulation"
(C.S. Lewis)

The only way out of the dark night, the trough, the silence, is through it.

Did God Abandon His Son?

"My God, my God, why have you forsaken me?"

Read Matthew 27:41-50.

• *"Eli, Eli, lema sabachthani?"* Jesus cried out loudly just moments before he succumbed to the Roman torture-execution that crucifixion was. The language was Aramaic—the common language of first-century Jews in Judea, and likely what Jesus spoke. Matthew the Gospel writer was kind enough to translate this for readers (as was Mark, in chapter 15)—which lets us recognize the error that some onlookers made when they heard this question that Jesus cried out in his agony.

• What did **these mistaken onlookers** believe Jesus had said?

• Do you feel that Jesus' **question was rhetorical?** That is, was he not as interested in an answer as he was simply expressing the agony of being abandoned? Or do you feel that he truly hoped for an answer from his Father?

• **What do you think it meant** for the Father to "forsake" his Son?

• Whatever you think it meant, *why* do you believe God forsook Jesus?

• Do you feel that God *actually, literally* forsook Jesus? Is that even possible? Talk about this.

• What was the **atmospheric situation between noon** and three? Do you think there was any connection between that and Jesus' question? Talk about this.

Finally...

• Anything in these verses that's a puzzle to you? That just doesn't make sense?

• What one thing got your attention most of all in these verses? Why did it affect you like it did?

---

⁴¹In the same way the chief priests, the teachers of the law and the elders mocked him. ⁴²"He saved others," they said, "but he can't save himself! He's the King of Israel! Let him come down now from the cross, and we will believe in him. ⁴³He trusts in God. Let God rescue him now if he wants him, for he said, 'I am the Son of God.'" ⁴⁴In the same way the robbers who were crucified with him also heaped insults on him. ⁴⁵From the sixth hour until the ninth hour darkness came over all the land. ⁴⁶About the ninth hour Jesus cried out in a loud voice, "Eloi, Eloi, lama sabachthani?" —which means, "My God, my god, why have you forsaken me?" ⁴⁷When some of those standing there heard this, they said, "He's calling Elijah." ⁴⁸Immediately one of them ran and got a sponge. He filled it with wine vinegar, and put it on a stick, and offered it to Jesus to drink. ⁴⁹The rest said, "Now leave him alone. Let's see if Elijah comes to save him." ⁵⁰And when Jesus had cried out again in a loud voice, he gave up his spirit.

—Matthew 27:41-50

Talk about the silence of the Lamb

• If God abandoned even his own Son at a time when Jesus needed him most, what stops God from abandoning us, too?

• In what sense have you ever felt abandoned by God? Do you believe it was your doing, or that it came out of the blue? Did you feel betrayed by God? Talk about this.

• Has God ever been silent when you most needed to hear from him? Talk about this. How was this a kind of abandonment?

• Why do you feel God can be silent when you most desperately want to hear from him?

• Respond to the following statements with YES, NO, or MAYBE SO:
 ~ I have been abandoned by God at least once in my life.
 ~ It is impossible to ever know why God seems to abandon a Christian.
 ~ If God is silent to someone, it's because that someone has sinned.
 ~ God never really abandons anyone who loves him—it only *seems* that way.

• If and when you're in a silent-God season, what help can it be to remember? Remember *what*?

Meeting of Minds

A conversation with Sarah, Moses, Mary Magdalene, and St. Luke

This is a roundtable conversation moderated by Barbara Walters (or whatever moderator you want). In front of the audience, set up a table and five chairs so that no actors sit with their backs to audience. Characters may dress per their era, in modern dress, or in something neutral (e.g, all characters except the moderator in black and white). This may be memorized or performed in readers' theater style, with or without rehearsal. It's best, of course, for readers at least to have read through it together once or twice before performing it. In a small group, of course, it won't be a performance, but an intimate reading with each other.

As the sketch opens, only the moderator is on stage. The guests enter on cue.

Barbara Walters: Tonight on "Meeting of Minds" we are flattered to have with us four individuals remarkable for coping with personal crisis.

Although Israeli-born, our first guest was a member of the Egyptian royal house during the 19th Dynasty. Personal circumstances forced him to flee the country, after which he lived in self-exile as a desert livestock manager—until his God Yahweh let him know in no uncertain terms that he was to return to Egypt and liberate Israel from Egyptian slavery. Welcome with me Moses, liberator and prophet of Israel.

Our next guest had an address in the red-light district of a Jerusalem suburb until she was rehabilitated by Jesus of Nazareth. She left her profession and became one of that messiah's many female disciples. This woman was with Jesus to the end—and beyond: it was to her, rather than to any of the inner circle of the messiah's twelve male disciples, that Jesus showed himself first when (it is claimed) he came back to life following his death by crucifixion. Ladies and gentlemen, please welcome Mary Magdalene.

Also joining us tonight is a man who was enlisted—or shall we say, converted?—to the retinue of Saul of Tarsus, known to Christians the world over as St. Paul. Trained in medicine, he also proved himself a gifted and insightful writer: his publishing credits include two New Testament books. In fact, he may have been the only non-Hebrew contributor to the New Testament. Physician, writer, traveler: let's welcome St. Luke.

Our fourth guest walked away from a very comfortable situation in one of the world's great cities, following her husband in what was to be a lifelong nomadic existence. A tiled floor and the pleasure of shopping the bazaars weren't the only pleasures denied her: she was infertile. Yet against all hope, in her old age she finally conceived and gave birth to her only son. Please welcome the "Mother of Nations," the grandmother of Israel himself: Sarah.

Let me say first of all, thank you all for breaking away and joining us tonight.

Moses, Sarah, Mary Magdalene, Luke: (*together*) Not at all...a pleasure to be here...just glad I was free tonight...good to be here...(*etc.*)

Barbara Walters: All of your stories are absolutely riveting, but Mary, I've got to say that yours hit me particularly hard. Which is strange, because happy endings don't usually affect me as much as yours did.

Mary Magdalene: It certainly *was* a happy ending, Barbara. But like most happy endings, it came—well, after a lot of wrong choices, after a lot of pain, after a lot of disappointment. In that sense, my story is no different from anyone's here—our five up here, or the audience's.

Sarah: Funny you should put it that way, Mary. My experience was just the opposite: my life was smooth, respectable, predictable—then a foreign God spoke to us, and *that's* when life started going south for me. Well, actually *west,* but you know what I mean.

Luke: (*gesturing to Moses*) Thanks to your storyteller over there, we do.

Sarah: (*nods and smiles toward Moses*) And my husband and I are forever grateful to him, too! But my misery started when Elohim, blessed be he, called us to leave our beautiful home in Ur and go to God knows where. *We* certainly didn't—not until we were standing on the land. Only then did Elohim say, "Here stake your tents. This is the land I promised you."

Moses: You make it sound like a gift on a silver platter.

Sarah: Well, you all know it wasn't. Elohim may have given that land to us, but we certainly had to negotiate for it, pay for it, fight for it, dig wells for our livestock in it—talk about the sweat equity we sunk into that land.

Moses: Not that I ever got there—to the land, that is. (*sighs*) It would have been welcome compensation for those 40-some years of frustration with my impulsive people. They forgot so much, so quickly.

Barbara Walters: Some would say you had a few impulsive moments of your own, Moses....

Moses: A reference to the deserved death of the Egyptian, no doubt.... Let it be known that I only defended the Jew he was beating to death. A man was going to die that afternoon, and, that time, I was able to prevent it being another Jewish death. (*pause*) Of course, the killing made me have to leave the country. Secretly, and in a hurry. One night I was sleeping on perfumed linen from the royal closets, and the next I was sleeping outside on rock and sand.

Luke: I spent more than a few nights camping outside like that, with Paul on his travels.

Moses: I spent a few *decades* living like this. And I had no reason to think that my life would ever be different. I was Egyptian nobility, and then I wasn't. I would spend the rest of my life as herdsman.

Mary Magdalene: But the bush that burned...

Moses: Yes, *that* certainly caught my attention. And it turned my life around once again. But what I remember the most as I knelt there for those moments or days—I could never figure out which it was...one never can, in the presence of God—anyway, there on my knees, Yahweh calling my name, I knew that I had never, really been alone. That when I fled Egypt, I had *not*— *could* not—flee from Yahweh. And this gave me hope. For there were dark days to come...and though I did my share of complaining, I never again really thought that Yahweh was far from me.

Mary Magdalene: Once I met Rabbi Jesus, I hardly ever *let* him leave me. Not many of his disciples did, once they had heard him.

Barbara Walters: Is that what attracted you? His teachings?

Mary Magdalene: Maybe that's what got my attention, and maybe it was something else...something about his tone of voice, or maybe his eyes. Whatever it was, there in the house, reclined at a meal, it just made me cry. I hadn't cried for ever so long...not many did, in that business. You have to be hard to work the streets.... You're hard and you earn money, or you die, one way or the other. Anyway, I started crying, there at the foot of his dining couch.... He told me later that he didn't hear anything, what caused him to turn and see me were my tears falling on his feet. Then I got embarrassed and, feeling like I had to do something, knelt and wiped his feet dry with my hair.

Luke: Tell them what he said, Mary...you know, about being forgiven....

Mary Magdalene: (*looking hard at Luke, though not unkindly*) How did you know that...?

Luke: (*with a wry grin*) I had my sources....

Mary Magdalene: Hmm...anyway, yes, when a synagogue leader got all hot and bothered about a woman like *me* touching him, the rabbi said, "She who has been forgiven much, loves much—and he who has been forgiven little, loves little." I had often thought of what it would take to get me off the streets...and that was the answer I needed.

Sarah: (*motherly, touching Mary Magdalene's arm*) That is such a dear memory.

Moses: (*half not understanding, half in awe of understanding, half to himself*) You saw the son of man with your own eyes...in flesh...and he looked into *your* eyes.... Who would have thought he would have been so...gentle.

Luke: Jesus could be tender as a mother. Although if the apostle Paul was any example, serving Jesus was seldom a tender experience. I swear, from the time I began following Jesus the messiah in Troas, till—

Barbara Walters: That would be in the nation we call Turkey today.

Luke: Ter-key? Whatever...anyway, in Troas I had a private practice in an aristocratic neighborhood. I was in the agora between house calls the day I heard the apostle Paul telling anyone who would listen about how the Hebrew God was now forgiving and accepting non-Jews, too—like me.

Moses: Foreigners have always been accepted into Israel, as long as they keep our law.... Haven't they?...

Luke: It's a long story, Prophet. Suffice it to say that by the time Jesus the son of man walked the roads of Canaan, Gentiles were pretty much shut out of faith—thanks, as usual, to the politics of control.

Barbara Walters: Let's jump ahead: you were with the apostle Paul to the end, weren't you?

Luke: Yes, I somehow stuck with him for the rest of his life—not a long one, as it turned out.

Paul seemed destined for deprivation—it seems I was always finding lodging next to the city jail, since he usually ended up there. I spent a lot of time and ointment patching him up after beatings by police or a mob. Funny...when he got into *serious* trouble—with Caesar, in Rome—I had a lot less work to do. Merely house arrest, no beatings, adequate food, visitors could come and go.

Sarah: But not a long life, you said?

Luke: Only two years in Rome before the emperor ran into political trouble, needed a scapegoat—

Moses: A scapegoat? So your *Gentile* emperor was sacrificing to Yahweh according to the law, then?

Luke: Uh? Oh, no—what I mean is...well—

Sarah: I can't recall that breed of goat among our herds. What does it look like?

Barbara Walters: I'll explain after the show, you two.

Luke: ...so Nero needed to pin the blame for some trouble of his own making on someone, and the Christians there in Rome were convenient. Paul was executed just outside the city limits. Several Roman Christians were with him at his death—Junia, Urbanus, Tryphena—I was, too.... You wouldn't believe how Paul encouraged us and blessed us before he knelt before the block....

Mary Magdalene: So much like our Lord, even in death. I, too, watched a man die whom I loved—a man who actually blessed his killers.

Barbara Walters: What kept you all from just folding emotionally, or giving up, in such dark circumstances?

Sarah: With me, it was remembering what Elohim, blessed be he, had told me earlier—even if I was skeptical at the time. The words of a God go deep, even if the hearer does not believe them at the time. "Sarah will have a son," I heard him say. That was all, but that was enough.

Mary Magdalene: The days after Rabbi Jesus' death were very hard, very dark, for all of his disciples. But I saw him when he left the tomb, and though he was not with us long after that even, the memory of seeing him alive again, flesh and blood, no mere ghost—well, such moments can keep one going for a long time. It did me.

Barbara Walters: Unfortunately, our moments here cannot. We must go. Mary, Sarah, Moses, Luke—thanks again for appearing on "Meeting of Minds." (*to audience*) Join our conversation next week with Samuel the Prophet, Pontius Pilate, Francis of Assisi, and Aimee Semple McPherson. Good night, everyone.

END